CLASSICAL ROME : POMPEII CIRCA A.D 50

CROSS SECTION X-X

SECTION SHOWING THE PAINTED WALL

Text within the drawing:

this wall painting is based on that by J.B. Martin as shown in fig 321 of the Hardwick D'Man

3 B
The Moon Garden

G.A. Jellicoe
17·2·88

The timber construction shown is conjectural. No cross bracing must be visible from the outside

PLAN, SECTION, ELEVATION OF THE TRELLIS ARCHWAY

6"   0'   1'   2'   3'   4   Scale of one foot to one inch

Detail: French Seventeenth Century. Trellis architecture with false perspective of Versailles

THE LANDSCAPE OF CIVILISATION

CREATED FOR

THE MOODY HISTORICAL GARDENS

DESIGNED AND DESCRIBED BY

GEOFFREY JELLICOE

GARDEN · ART · PRESS

ISBN 1 870673 01 8

British Library Cataloguing-in-Publication Data:
A catalogue record for this book is available from the British Library

Printed on Consort Royal Satin from Donside Mills, Aberdeen

Endpapers
Front: Islam and Classical Rome as detailed
Back: Egypt and the Bridge as detailed

Published by Garden Art Press
a division of Antique Collectors' Club

Printed in England by the Antique Collectors' Club Ltd, Woodbridge, Suffolk IP12 1DS

CONTENTS

continued

continued

COLOUR PLATES

(Drawings, paintings and photographs. **Bold** references are to the author's own numbered drawings)

THE CHALLENGE

The site is not congenial to man. The salt marshes that teem with an independent life of their own, will not invite him. Although he is conquering space at the near by Houston Space Centre, he will remain on planet earth harassed by winds, hurricanes and inundations. Without destroying either wild life or himself can he implant permanently into this extraordinary scene the marvellous story of his use from it? He can but try and indeed should, for:

The greatest threat to man's existence may not be commercialism, or war, or pollution, or noise, or consumption of capital resources, or even the threat of extinction from without, but rather the blindness that follows sheer lack of appreciation and the consequent destruction of those values in history that together are symbolic of a single great idea.

Landscape of Man

THE RESPONSE

The model was made in Galveston. In the foreground are the civilisations of the west; in the middle distance the mountain divide; in the distance the civilisations of the east.

The straight sea wall in the foreground was determined by the adjoining partly-used airfield. The peculiar line of the protective earth dyke was determined by the natural division of dry and wet lands. The internal space has the characteristic of a sunk garden.

The model emphasises that an exact botanical specification has yet to be made, a work complementary to this volume and now in preparation.

FOREWORD

Sir Hugh Casson CH, KCVO, PPRA, RDI Architect

This remarkable book is the summary of a noble idea and an illustrated account of its progress towards its physical expression. It is the work of a remarkable and deeply modest man — architect, planner, landscape designer, teacher, scholar and philosopher — internationally celebrated within his own fields of study but to the general public still largely unknown. His concept, matured and enriched by sixty years of teaching, study and practice, is the history of mankind from myth through humanism to the disorientation of the present-day, interpreted and expressed through the design of gardens and landscape.

The chosen place for presenting this story in sequence from the Garden of Eden to the end of the nineteenth century is a marsh in Galveston, Texas, and work will soon begin on site. Visitors will be able either to travel by boat or to explore the gardens on foot, but their voyage through time and space is intended to be more than just a spectacle. En route it will identify and comment upon the use of symbolism and the release of the subconscious, the observation of natural forms and the contribution of tyrants, the balance of logic and caprice, of fear and pleasure, of those experiences that can only be sensed in the imagination.

To the English — always nervous in the presence of bold concepts — this may seem heady stuff — but the simplicity, sensitivity and irresistible delicacy of the drawings that accompany the thesis will instantly reassure and inspire the reader to go and see these gardens for himself or herself.

In times of cultural unease man has always turned for help to the four familiar marker buoys of religion, art, scholarship and nature. Geoffrey Jellicoe reminds us that in landscape and gardens all these elements can be found and studied and enjoyed. Here, he suggests, will be found perhaps that mixture of myth and humanism, of beauty and order, of mystery and delight, which will in the end, perhaps, help us to find reassurance and inspiration in our lives.

Hugh Casson
President of the Royal Academy 1976-84

Aerial view of the Moody Gardens complex looking west, taken in 1988. On the left, in the middle distance beyond the inlet, is seen the twenty year building programme of the complex well advanced. On the right in the far distance between the straight road and sea, is seen the site of the Historical Gardens, scheduled to begin in the early 1990s

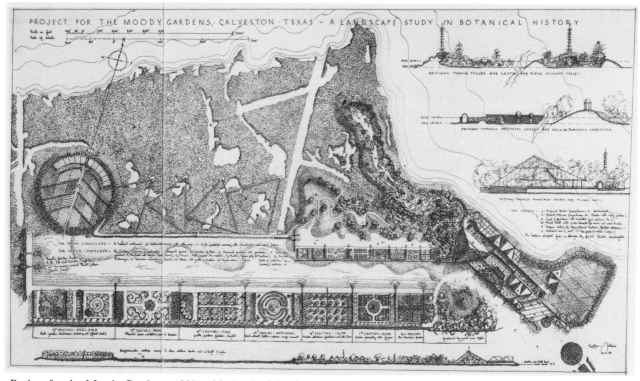

Project for the Moody Gardens, 1985, with detail of the Classical sequence

INTRODUCTION

Peter Atkins, Director of Horticulture, The Moody Gardens

Moody Gardens is a tribute to the people of Texas. Through the benefaction of The Moody Foundation this botanical garden is being developed in Galveston, Texas. The concept for the overall master plan of this 142-acre botanical garden, located on a barrier island, has been developed since initial meetings in 1982. When the inception of the idea of a botanical garden began, the Trustees of The Moody Foundation were Mrs Mary Moody Northen, the Chairman of the Board, and her two nephews, Mr Shearn Moody, Jr, and Mr Robert Lee Moody. Although a total team approach is present, the concept of the botanical facet of the garden was due to the desires and inspirations of Mr Shearn Moody, Jr, whereas the therapeutic commitment of the overall complex should be attributed to his brother, Mr Robert Lee Moody.

The evolution of the programming for Moody Gardens has always been tied to the mandate that this uniquely modern garden complex is to be financially self-sufficient. This is an extraordinary feat for a traditionally public garden. Therefore, much effort has been made to ensure that financial stability be attained. During the early spring of 1983, one year after initial development meetings took place in Galveston, I made contact with Sir Geoffrey Jellicoe. Our meeting included Susan (Lady Jellicoe), Charles and Myra Funke, and my wife Susan. The purpose of the proposed botanical garden project, later to be called Moody Gardens, was discussed, along with the creation of basic philosophical understandings between Sir Geoffrey and myself.

The next development was Sir Geoffrey's visit to the United States, when he visited with two of the Trustees, Shearn and his brother Robert. We also visited Disney World and the special features of EPCOT Center, located near Orlando, Florida, both of which can be referred to as successful public attractions. That initial trip set the stage for what was to become the major garden emphasis at Moody Gardens. The basic question arose as to what could Moody Gardens have as its basic core that would not only create Moody Gardens as a destination facility but could benefit the general visitor by being an educational facility?

Galveston Island is an island located off the southeast coast of Texas. The people on this subtropical island are tenacious and extremely proud of their heritage, guarding it with fervor. The thought developed that a botanical garden which would expose local residents and visitors to the wonders of landscape, horticulture and botany could not only be an enchancement to the quality of life of Galvestonians and the immediate region, but could also attract distant people to this paradise island. Therefore, the concept of a botanical garden that is a destination facility was beginning to emerge with specific reference to worldly exposure associated with beauty and enjoyment. These concepts were going to be the mission statement of Moody Gardens.

In May 1985, a design meeting took place in Seattle, Washington, under the auspices of E Douglas McLeod, the Director of Development of The Moody Foundation, and Chairman of The Development Team. Those present included: the late Don Palmer, from Las Vegas; Bios, from Seattle, Washington; Sir Geoffrey Jellicoe, from Great Britain, and me, from Duke University, Durham, North Carolina. This momentous occasion modified an initial and most extraordinary grand design which Sir Geoffrey envisioned while in Great Britain, into a botanical garden that was probably a bit more in keeping with the mission statement mandating financial self-sufficiency. What evolved was the concept of the Historic Gardens — tracing man's use of the landscape from the beginning of time through the nineteenth century.

Finalization of the concept, then lead to minor revolutionary tweakings or fine tunings of the design, involving the services of Smith Locke Asakura, landscape architects, and Morris Architects. A presentation was made to Trustees of The Moody Foundation. Their reaction was enthusiastic and there seemed to be an accord with what had evolved. It became apparent to those working on the project that Moody Gardens could potentially become The Moody Foundation's thumb print on the world. Their legacy to the people of Texas, in the form of a botanical garden, could be one of the most beautiful educational facilities ever produced.

What is before us in this book is more than the culmination of a great man's career. I believe that it contains Sir Geoffrey Jellicoe's conceptualization of how man has evolved and demonstrates this concept through landscape. The purpose is: not just to give the visitor the feeling of history; not just to show beauty; not just the thrill of being close to waterfalls and the immediate excitement of the fragrances and wonders of a botanical garden. But, hopefully, what the visitor will get is something that heretofore he or she has never experienced. The true ethos, the true meaning of what we are about to put into the ground, is a demonstration of the philosophies of civilizations from the beginning through the nineteenth century. This has never been done before in a botanical setting.

All the benefactors, designers, staff, contractors and visitors, to this date, seem to feel that being associated with Moody Gardens is a very unique experience. It conjures up the ideas and the feelings associated with the meaningfulness of a mission. A mission that implies a sacrifice upon all individuals to make sure that the entire program is realized. This implies very strong commitments to therapy, beauty, education and excellence. This sense of purpose is pervasive over the entire project; from the design through the implementation, and to the maintenance of a fantastic garden complex.

The attempt is to create an experience that is greater than life. The individual, although extraordinarily important, is not the basis of this garden. The basis of the garden is the concept that the individual is but a very minute part of the entire cosmos. The visitor will be exposed to a landscape that will hopefully generate feelings from within that will play upon the subconscious.

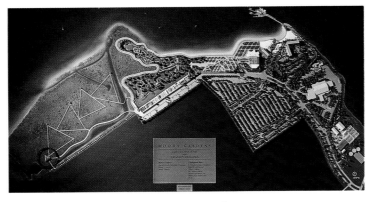

The total plan of the Moody garden complex

Section from model showing China

It will hopefully make him or her a better person. Our aim has been to enhance the quality of life for all who pass through the gates of Moody Gardens.

I would like to close this introduction with a very personal note. It has been an extraordinary experience to work with Sir Geoffrey Jellicoe, for he has had a great effect upon my life. He has exposed me to new thoughts and perceptions that I had not previously considered. It has been a joy to work with The Moody Foundation, the Moody Gardens' staff, and those designers, contractors and visitors who have been involved with Moody Gardens. To be part of such a wonderful project has made me a better person. I am not alone with this feeling, for it seems that everyone who has been part of this development, demonstrates such zealous fanaticism and concern for detail; a concern about being sure that not only our direction is clearly defined, but that we strive to assure its eventual realization and completion. This could not have been accomplished without the concepts of Sir Geoffrey Jellicoe and the far reaching visions, dedications and continuing courage of the Trustees of The Moody Foundation.

Director of Horticulture
Moody Gardens

PLACE AND PROJECT

This is a guide to the designs for the Historical Gardens that will form part of the Moody Gardens at Galveston. The work on the gardens is planned to begin in 1992, giving time for the further preparatory studies that are essential to make them the most scholarly as well as most dramatic of their kind in garden history. The challenge is indeed breathtaking: to compress the experience of a time scale of three thousand years and the space scale of the globe into a time scale of a few hours and a space scale of twenty-five acres. Clearly it cannot be done through realism; so it is being tried through surrealism or the projection of the *idea* or essence of a culture.

The story of how and why the gardens were conceived is unique.

Galveston Island in the Gulf of Mexico lies two miles off the coast of Texas, some fifty miles south of Houston (below). Thirty miles long and averaging two miles in width, it acts as a barrier reef to the mainland and provides a remarkable natural harbour. Originally little more than a windswept sand bar, with scrub oaks and the like, civilised history began when a Spanish explorer landed here in 1528. In 1685 it was claimed by the French. In 1786 it became Spanish under the governor Bernardo de Galvez, after whom it was named. In 1817 it was Venezuelan, in 1821 Mexican, and in 1836 it became part of the Republic of Texas. Texas joined the Union in 1845 and the Confederacy in 1861. In 1868 slavery was abolished by proclamation and in the following year Colonel William Lewis Moody (1828-1920), a native of Virginia, settled here with his family to help create one of the most prosperous cities in America. Then, on 8th September 1900, came disaster with the virtual destruction of the city by hurricane and inundation.

In the worst natural disaster in North American history six thousand persons lost their lives, many of the population of 38,000 fled to the mainland never to return, and the city was left in ruins. Its economy was destroyed and its place as the commercial centre of southern Texas was taken by Houston. Nevertheless, as with so many cities destroyed in war, the ethos of the place was, and still is, so strong that those of the original inhabitants who survived

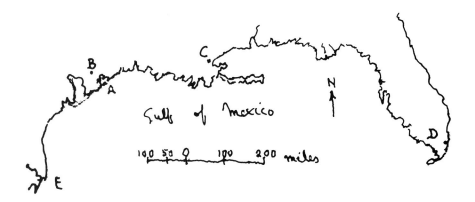

Location of Galveston in the Gulf of Mexico

A Galveston Island
B Houston
C New Orleans
D Miami
E Boundary with Mexico

Plan of site
A Moody Gardens
B Offatts Bayou
C Airfield
D Suburbs
E Bridge and approach from
   Houston from which
   outstanding views of
   the garden are seen
F Railway bridge.
G Broadway to City centre
H Sea wall

(BOI — Born on the Island — remains a proud term) set out on the prodigious work of reconstruction. Unlike cities destroyed in war which could not foresee the tactics of future attack, the Galvestonians knew precisely the powers of the enemy and planned accordingly in a manner that is itself an epic. The city on average was raised twelve feet above the existing three feet above sea level, a task involving dredging within the island itself and the total realignment of services. Elsewhere by law all new buildings on the island were to be built on stilts with a minimum of fifteen feet above sea level. The huge sea wall and boulevard, now extending ten and a half miles along the south shore facing the Gulf, was virtually completed by 1910, reputedly the most formidable of its kind in the world. Further hurricanes and inundations have caused little damage to building, but Hurricane Alice in August 1983 was particularly destructive of the vegetation that, ever since oleanders were introduced in the early nineteenth century, had been painstakingly developed by individual efforts.

Today the modern city with a population of 62,000, a special interest in conservation of the past and a rapidly growing tourist trade, has an air of prosperity. But it is deficient in vegetation, exceptions proving that trees and shrubs and flowers can flourish given encouragement and the properly sheltered environment. The establishment therefore of these gardens in an area naturally hostile to plants will be both a challenge to the elements and an immense stimulus to the island as a whole.

The location of the gardens lies on what may be described as the soft under belly of the island (opposite), on an inlet of the north shore known as Offatts Bayou, a long narrow strip, partly of wet-lands or marshes wedged between an airfield and the sea (above). The wet-lands are strictly wildlife preserves and account for the baroque shape into which the historical gardens will be fitted. The total length of over a mile is divided roughly into three parts: the *east* includes the already constructed Hope Arena and Conference Hall, and proposed hotel, quay for pleasure steamers, foreshore plage, restaurants and other pleasantries leading to the educational campus with glass houses and theatre. The *centre* contains the Historical Gardens described in this guide. To the *west* are the walkways beyond the dyke, seen skipping across the wet-lands to the great dyke-protected circle of the nursery.

The most comfortable and briefest way of seeing the Historical Gardens is the one chosen for this guide — the water-bus. This is only intended, however, to whet the appetite and invite a visit on foot along the two miles of paths. A serious study could take two days or more. Although the whole is intended to be a single surrealistic picture, it is also intended to be academically correct in spirit and in detail. It is sound, therefore, that the opening is not for some years, for the research that follows these drawings (made to a scale of eight feet to one inch) will be considerable. Consider plants, for instance, which on the drawings are only shown suggestively. First there must be a study of what plants were likely to be in use at any one period. Then that they are available today and, if not, the selection made of an alternative. After this there must be at least a two year period to see if the species can be acclimatised. On the data thus known there now follows the making of an aesthetic planting plan. Finally comes the planting process itself on previously prepared sites.

By far the most difficult part of this exercise has been the basic choice of subject, disposition, proportions and neighbourliness of all the various cultures. The composition for the whole peculiar site resolved itself without a struggle. The straight line marking the boundary with the airfield suggested the geometry of classicism; the short middle of the site suggested the great divide between west and east; eighteenth century European romanticism, so important to the modern world, filled the shapes on the further side of the classical waters; China and Japan were equally accommodating to the long narrow space in which they had to be contained.

No study of history can be absolute when interpreted through the research of an individual. No two historians will think precisely alike. It is, for instance, this designer's own view that landscape classicism can be compressed into a box (like Shakespeare's Globe), but that romanticism cannot and that the styles which quarrelled in history need not do so today.

The concept of the gardens is that they are a projection into space, up to the nineteenth century, of my own and my wife's *Landscape of Man,* first published in 1975.

The reader, unlike the voyager in reality, must forgive the presentation in draughtsman's rectangles. These were devised prior to the idea of a written guide and will ultimately be pieced together in a four-metre square on the wall of Reception.

Geoffrey Jellicoe
Highpoint, London, 1987

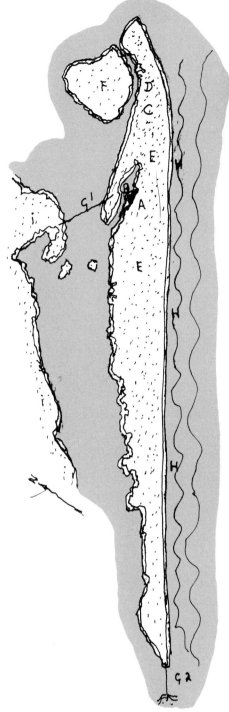

Galveston Island showing
location of Moody Gardens
A Moody Gardens
B Offatts Bayou
C City centre
D Docks
E Suburbs
F Pelican Island
G1 Bridge to mainland and
    Houston,
G2 Bridge to mainland
H Sea wall
I Mainland

Original sketch for the gardens made overnight in the hotel bedroom and presented to Peter Atkins and others at Seattle 19.5.85

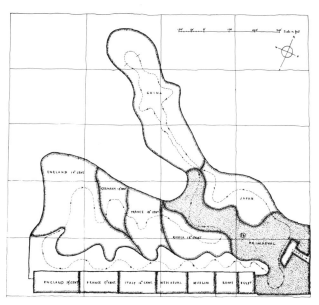

The plan as developed from the sketch, showing the areas of the primary civilisations

THE ALLOCATION OF SPACE

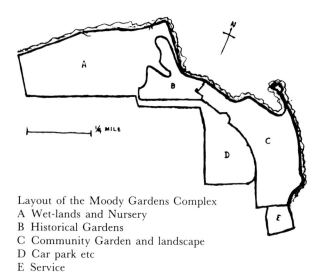

Layout of the Moody Gardens Complex
A Wet-lands and Nursery
B Historical Gardens
C Community Garden and landscape
D Car park etc
E Service

The SITE is slightly above sea level. The approach is from the campus to the east. On the south it is bounded by the straight line of the airfield. The irregular shape to north and west was governed by wildlife restrictions of the wet-lands. The whole is surrounded by a twelve foot dyke or wall as protection against inundation. The area falls naturally into three parts: the WESTERN and EASTERN cultures separated, as they are on the planet, by the PRIMAEVAL.

The drawing opposite is approximately twelve feet square and for convenience of drafting has been divisioned into the fourteen rectangles (inadvertently detrimental to China and Japan) that follow. The space for China is proportionate to the three thousand years and more of its landscape history.

The PLAN is composed of the 'essence' of historic gardens and landscapes. Each 'essence' is not so much the copy of an actual example as the abstract idea, academically executed, that seems best to represent the age. The WESTERN CULTURES, predominantly *secular,* fall into two categories: classical and romantic. The classical sequence, expressive of the geometry and rhythms of the heavens, represents stability and rational thought in a world of

Waterbus : suggested sub-campus location for embarkation, repairs, storage, etc

200' 50' 0'   100'   200'   300' Scale in feet

Overall plan showing the rectangles of the original drawings, numbered 1-14, pieced together to form an approx 12ft square on the walls of Reception

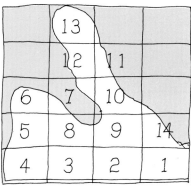

Numbered route of the water-bus

turmoil; it is accepted that a great and tranquil idea through mathematical proportion can be contained in a finite box. In contrast, the romanticism of eighteenth century Europe, the basis of the future public park, derives from the irrational in man and his urge to return to uninhibited nature: thus the boundless spaces which create further spaces beyond the eye. The EASTERN CULTURES are basically *metaphysical* and philosophically static. Some two thousand years of Chinese culture is dominated by the Buddha; the Japanese Zen garden is the deepest visual expression ever made of man's struggle to *feel* his relation to infinity.

PART 1

THE VOYAGE

Being the description of the route on water
through the Historical Gardens

TO THE READER

The voyage through time and space that you are about to undertake is not as topsy-turvy nor as human and humorous as that of *Alice in Wonderland* but the principle is the same. The world that you will experience is in three levels of unreality. The first is that you must regard the drawings much as Alice regarded the looking glass, as something to pass through to reach the world of imagination that lies beyond. The second unreality will be to enjoy sensuously those things that you must conjure up in your imagination, not only from what is shown on paper but all the multitude of unseen delights of eye and ear — trees, flowers, architecture, follies, sculpture, fountains, cascades, mountains, cliffs, grottoes, and the changing yet unchanging waters that run like 'the thread of truth' (as the poet says) through all civilisation. The third unreality, that of a metaphysical experience, may not strike you until some time after your return.

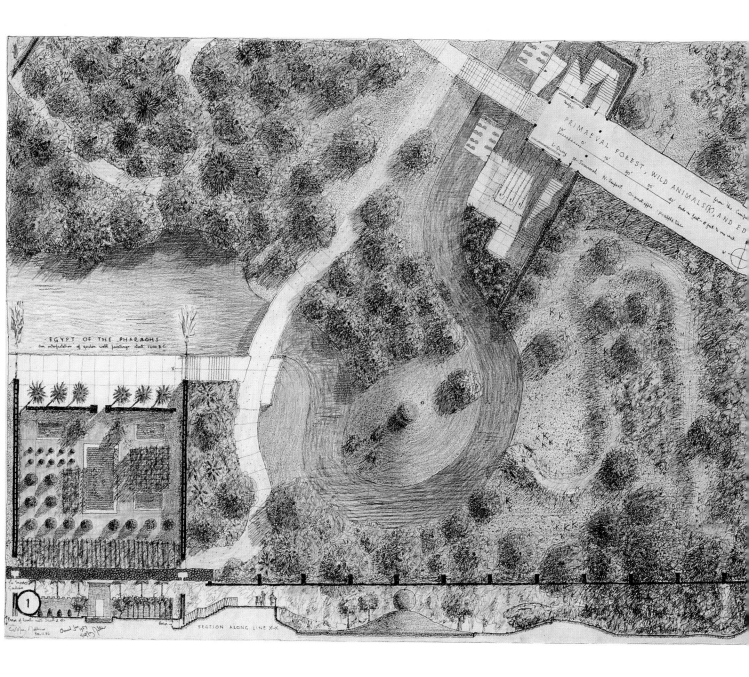

Within the illustration, handwritten labels are visible, including:

PRIMAEVAL FOREST, WILD ANIMALS(K), AND ED...

EGYPT OF THE PHARAOHS
An interpretation of garden wall paintings about 1400 B.C.

SECTION ALONG LINE X-X

The Western Culture —
the Beginning of Classicism

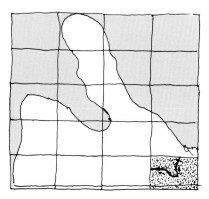

The route of the water-bus. Primaeval
Forest; Eden; Egypt

EDEN

We board the water-bus at the foot of the stairway leading from the campus.
On the left there soon appears the primaeval savannah with wild animals,
dominated by a sinister rock with a long slimy rear. Then, on the right, a soft
green slope announces Eden, symbolised by the giant Apple that has fallen
from the Tree of Knowledge. We navigate the hill and, westward of Eden,
confront the grand perspective of the seven decisive cultures of the classical

world, separated by cascades of water upon which they have all depended. In the far distance we see the two inquisitive giants peering over the wall from outer space.

EGYPT

As the boat moves at pedestrian speed past Egypt and you see nothing except a high wall behind palms and a glimpse through the entrance doorway, you realise that this voyage can sometimes do no more than rouse your curiosity. We, however, are not so constrained, quitting the boat to enter a patio garden that almost certainly signifies the birth of the small classical garden. The place is Thebes, the time about 1500 BC.

Conditions were ripe for such an event. The previous absolutism of the Pharaohs had softened into a mixed society that had easily absorbed slavery. With external peace and internal tranquillity plus a Nile that delivered free goods on time, and with the glorious avenue of sphinx leading from Karnak to the first ever terraces of Queen Hatshepsut, Thebes as the capital of the New Kingdom (the XVIIIth Dynasty) may claim to be the first truly landscape city of the western world (right).

This garden of a prosperous citizen — an imaginary design based on limited data — is contained within either granite or mud-baked walls that ensure privacy and protection against marauders, human or animal. The primary needs were water supplied abundantly in buckets by slaves, and shade through trellis, pergola, arbour and other features. Because it was intensely personal and the age was loosening up, the traditional strict symmetry has been modified to the taste of the imaginary owner. Probably not until the Middle Ages was there such acute sensitivity towards nature. The garden was aesthetic and it was practical. It provided fresh fruit for the household, such as the indigenous vine or pomegranate and the imported apple and almond, and fresh fish in the lotus-covered pools (larger gardens would have water tanks for angling and reclining in awning-covered boats, with wild ducks). Sycamore, date palms, down palms and smaller trees are planted geometrically, but native and imported flowers are in informally placed earthenware pots. Garden and owner were as one, seemingly in the next world as well as this.

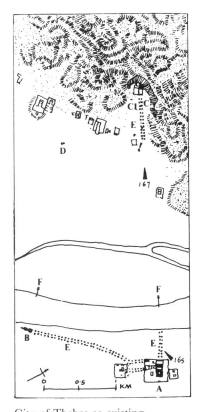

City of Thebes as existing
A Temple of Ammon, Karnak
B Temple of Ammon, Luxor
C Tomb of Hatshepsut
D Colossi of Memnon
E Avenue of Sphinxes
F Crossings of River Nile

Egyptian fishing

In a certain sense gardens were always held sacred by Egyptians. Indeed, everything any man did had a religious significance for what he accomplished in this life was of immediate utility to his soul on the other side. Every private person sought, above all things, if it were in any way feasible, to put shady trees round his home; for what he planted here — to enjoy the shade and to bathe in the perfume of its flowers — was really an act of thoughtful kindness to his soul. In times of heat his soul will be able to step forth from the grave wherein it dwells, and enjoy the cooling shade. The inscriptions on the tombs lay stress on this idea: 'That each day I may walk on the banks of my water, that my soul may repose on the branches of the trees I have planted, that I may refresh myself under the shadow of my sycamore'.
From *History of Garden Art,* Marie Luise Gothein

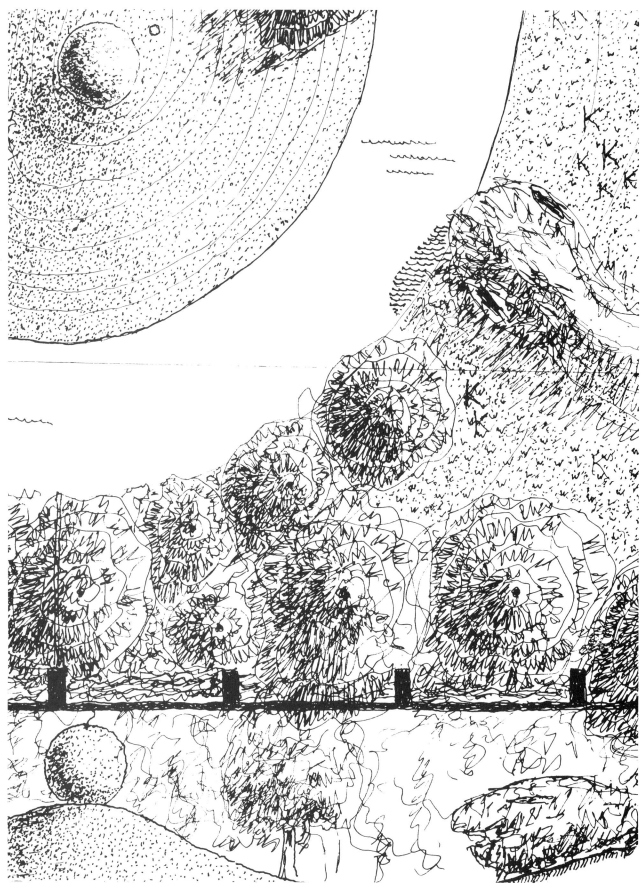

Moss Apple and the sinister rock

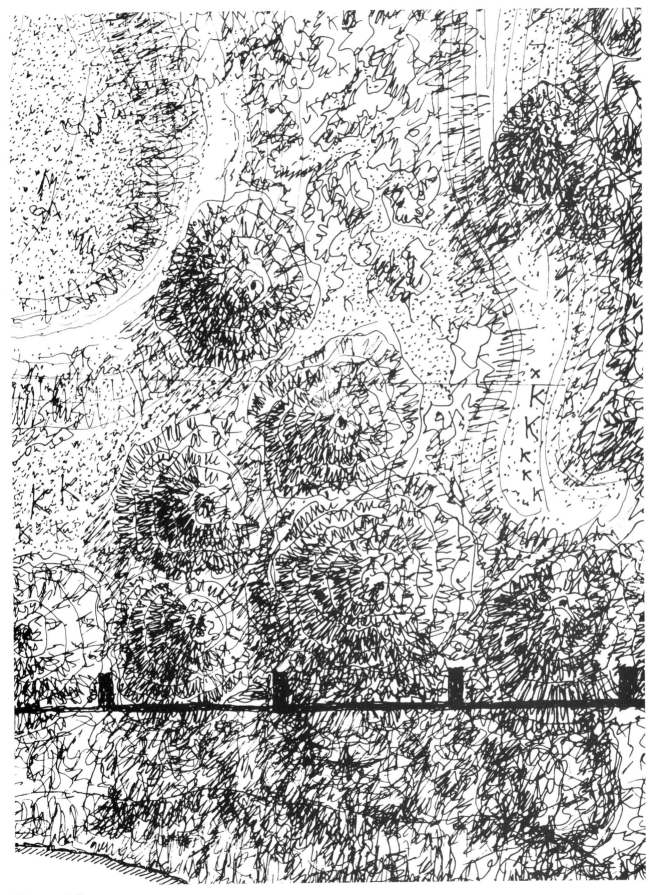

Primaeval Forest

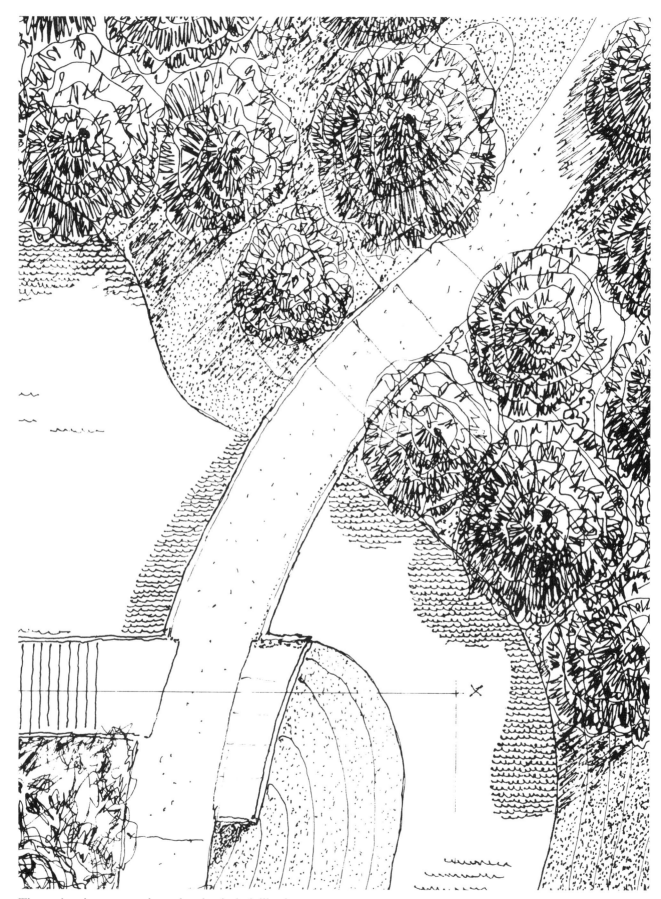

The pedestrian approach to the classical civilisations

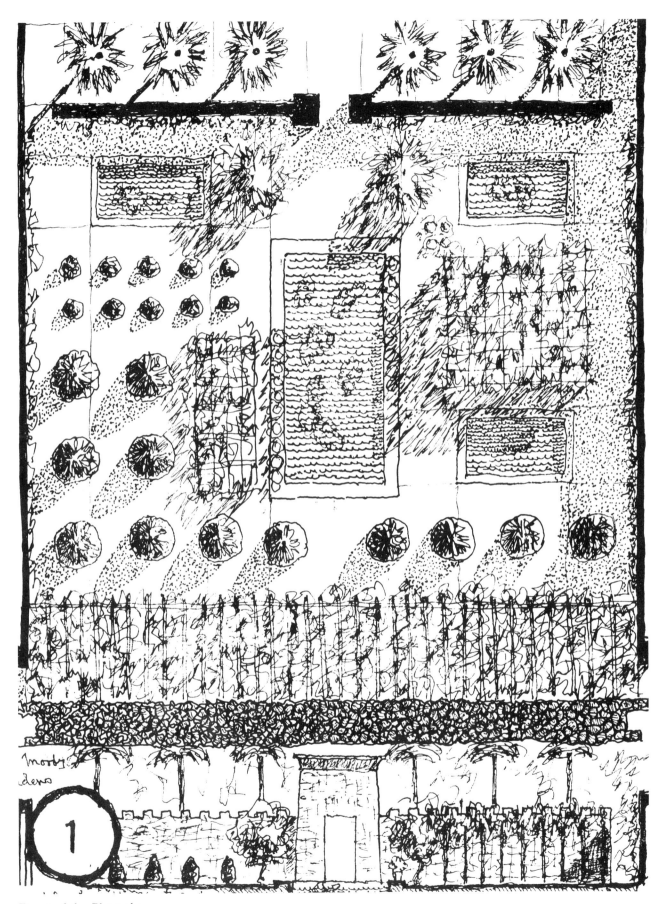

Egypt of the Pharaohs

The Western Culture — Classical Rome, Islam, Mediaeval Europe

ROME

Fifteen hundred years or so separate the Thebes of the XVIIIth Dynasty from Imperial Rome. While pure philosopy plus water shortage in Greece discouraged the making of gardens, Greco-Roman Alexandria seems to have inspired perhaps the most humane Roman achievement in landscape design: the small urban garden. Set against the huge slave-maintained layouts described by Pliny the Younger, and at the heart of a mighty empire that had stamped its personality on the furthest colony (below left), the Pompeian garden is unique. The city was buried by the eruption of Vesuvius in AD 79, but enough survived from the lava to allow reconstruction.

Statistically the garden we see only briefly from the water-bus has the same dimensions and proportions as the House of the Vettii (below right), but the presentation had been adjusted to suit the conditions. Although the principle of privacy is similar to that of Egypt, the philosophic and social use is fundamentally different. Whereas the Egyptian entered the garden to become part of it, the Pompeian regarded it as something to be observed from the shady peristyle that surrounded it on all four sides.

There would be little outstanding about the Pompeian garden, charming though it is with its fountains, rivulets, pools, miniature sculptures and flowers of all kinds, were it not for the paintings that cover the walls of the peristyle. Space is extended through a form of landscape surrealism, appealing as much

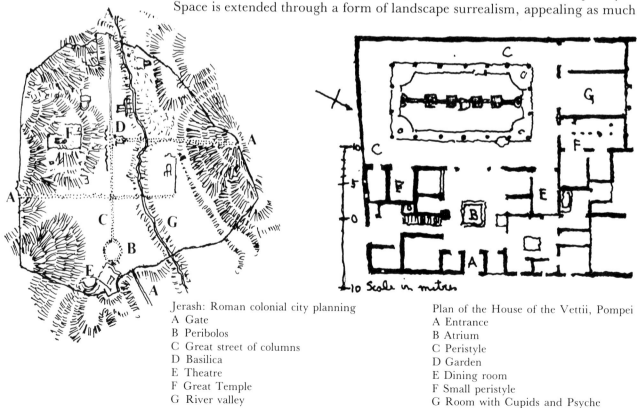

Jerash: Roman colonial city planning
A Gate
B Peribolos
C Great street of columns
D Basilica
E Theatre
F Great Temple
G River valley

Plan of the House of the Vettii, Pompei
A Entrance
B Atrium
C Peristyle
D Garden
E Dining room
F Small peristyle
G Room with Cupids and Psyche

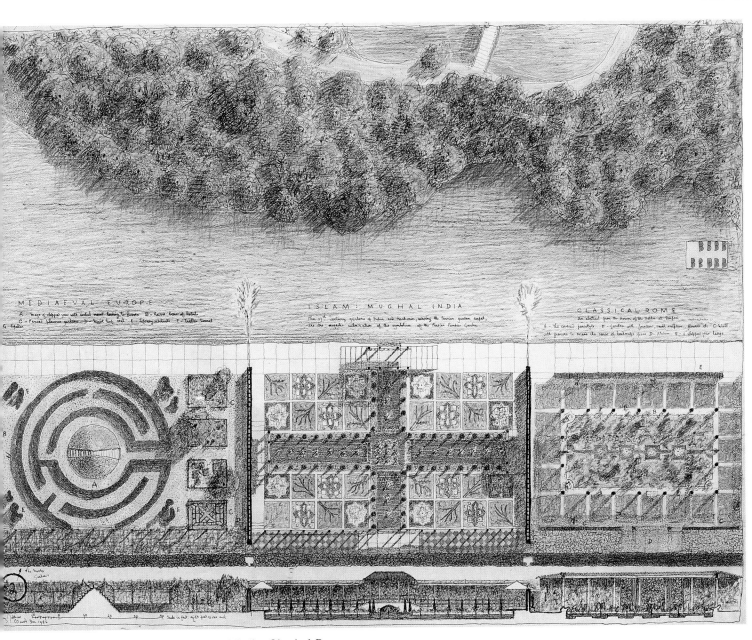

Mediaeval Europe; Islam: Mughal India; Classical Rome

to the mind as the eye. Through such illusion this small urban plot contains the *idea* of the grandeur of classical Rome, together with Greece the founder of western civilisation.

ISLAM

The landscape history of Islam has been independent of the classical west, but interwoven with it. It began in Mesopotamia with the Biblical river flowing out of Eden and parting into four rivers of life. In due time and inspired by the straight irrigation channels between the Tigris and Euphrates, the symbolic Persian Paradise garden was evolved, so called by the Greeks. This was all-square, geometrical and walled against a hostile world, with cross canals to fertilise plants of all kinds. After Persia had fallen to Alexander, the Sassanids revived the dynasty in AD 226 and it was then that the famous Spring Carpet of Chosrues II, a hundred feet long, became one of the glories of the capital Ctesiphon. The twin ideas of symbolism and that a carpet can be a garden,

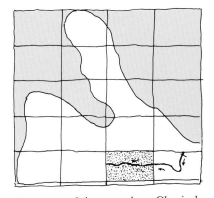

The route of the water-bus. Classical Rome; Islam: Mughal India; Mediaeval Europe

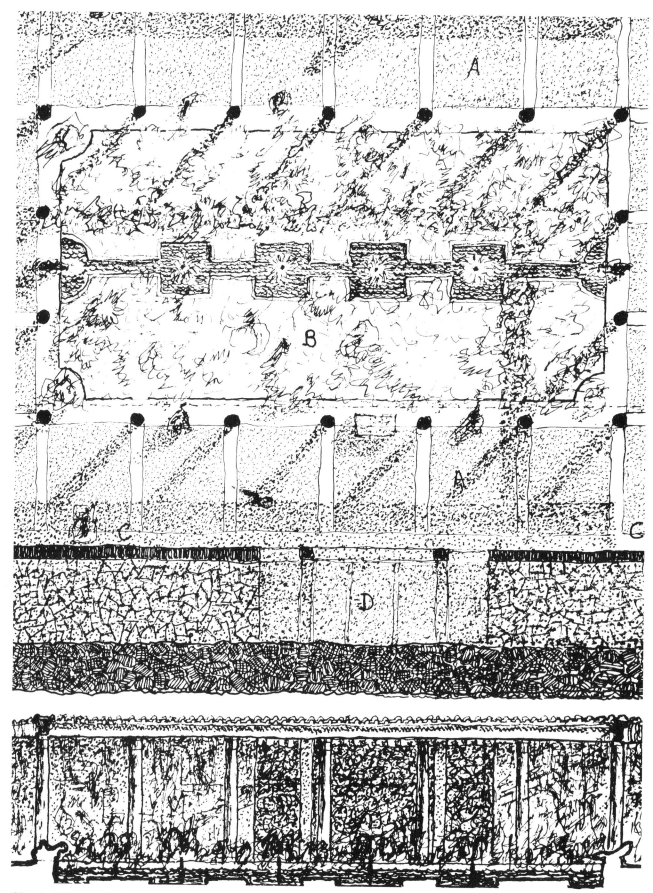

Classical Rome: the house of the Vettii, Pompei

Islam: Mughal India

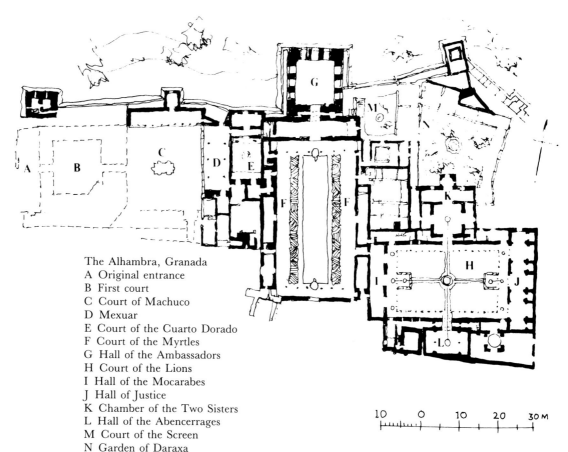

The Alhambra, Granada
A Original entrance
B First court
C Court of Machuco
D Mexuar
E Court of the Cuarto Dorado
F Court of the Myrtles
G Hall of the Ambassadors
H Court of the Lions
I Hall of the Mocarabes
J Hall of Justice
K Chamber of the Two Sisters
L Hall of the Abencerrages
M Court of the Screen
N Garden of Daraxa

10   0   10   20   30 M

The Shalimar Bagh, Kashmir, as existing
A Canal approach from Lake Dal
B Curtailed court or public garden
C The Emperor's Garden
D Ladies' Garden

or vice-versa, was established long before Islam.

When the Prophet Mahomet fanatically conquered Persia in AD 637 the conquerors absorbed the spirit of Persian art. The centre was Baghdad but the influence spread east and west. In the east it culminated in Mughal India, the Taj Mahal and the impressive mountain gardens of Kashmir (left) (see Appendix: Jung and the Magic Mountain). In the west it culminated in the Alhambra in Spain (above), captured by the Christians in 1492, having infused indelible ideas into both the European Middle Ages and the Italian Renaissance. The exhibition garden itself is the transformation into reality of a seventeenth century carpet that derives from the original Spring Carpet, the source of Islamic design.

MEDIAEVAL EUROPE

Europe of the middle ages was less tolerant than Islam. The illiterate, who far out-numbered the literate, were taught by an international and brilliantly organised religion to believe blindly that the good life led to Heaven and the evil to the fires of Hell. No mediaeval gardens exist, but from what is recorded in pictures and tapestries the ladies' castle gardens in particular must have been exquisite — fountains, flowers, knots, arbours, herbs for the kitchen. The true symbol of the age, however, and dominating the exhibition garden, must assuredly be the maze, the groping towards a heaven not easy to reach. Beside the maze stand ominous figures in topiary, to protect the pilgrim and spur the waverer. (Changed to the twelve apostles attending the Sermon on the Mount, see detail page 152).

Mediaeval mysteries and castle gardens

P E

B — Raised beds of herbals
Topiary abstracts   F — Trellis tunnel

For details of the water walls between the civilisations, see page 190

The Western Culture — the Italian Renaissance, the French Seventeenth Century

THE ITALIAN RENAISSANCE

To pass from mediaevalism to Italy of the Renaissance is to pass from the irrational to the rational, from gloom to sun. Man emerged for the first time in history as an individual capable of reasoning for himself, suddenly awake to the beauty of the world about him. He saw himself as the centre of the universe and for a short while revelled in this and many another meditation on the nobility of self.

The saga of the Italian garden is richer and more varied than any other garden culture, falling roughly into three periods: the True Renaissance (1400-1500) (right); the High Renaissance (1500-1600) and Mannerism and Baroque (1600-1700) (below). Although the actual awakening took place in Florence, it was in Rome that the first serious studies were made of the ruins of antiquity and the startling discovery of proportion as an echo of the rational human mind.

So it is that, leaving behind mysticism and the charm of flowers, we shall again go on shore to let the mind unconsciously absorb what the eye cannot: the divine gift of mathematics. Nor need we worry about this intellectualism for even from the boat the scene of an imagined garden of the High Renaissance is seductive to the senses: the mythological caryatids, the long shady airy arcade, the tremendous folly, the splendid carpet patterned in evergreens and fountains, the music and sparkle of rising and falling waters, and the dignity and grandeur of it all.

Yet beneath this placid surface of civilisation lay the seeds of decay, epitomised by the monster of the Villa Orsini, Bomarzo — unseen from the boat, but surfacing to frighten the timid in the detailed drawings on pages 40, 162 and 165.

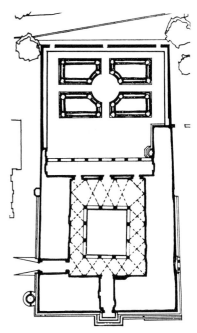

Piccolomini Palace, Pienza.
A design of the True Renaissance

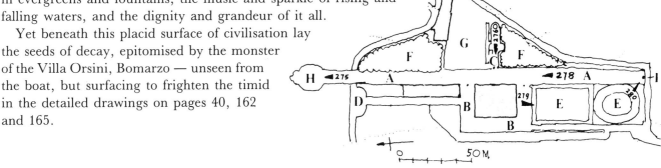

Villa Gamberaia, near Florence,
an example of mannerism
A Long gallery
B Grass view terrace
C Grotto garden
D Entrance drive
E Original water garden
F Bosco
G Lemon garden
H Cypress garden
I Statue on view point

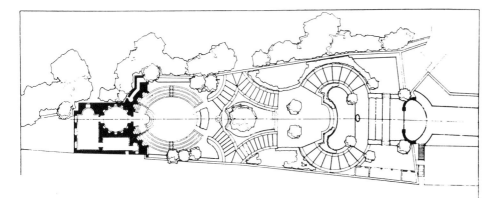

The Arcadian Academy, Rome. An example of Italian Baroque

37

The French Seventeenth Century; the Italian Sixteenth Century

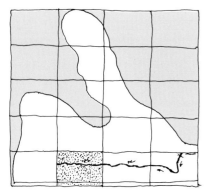

The route of the water-bus. The Italian Sixteenth Century; the French Seventeenth Century

FRANCE

The Renaissance in France began in 1496 with the return of Charles VIII from Italy to his home at Amboise in the Loire valley. During the next century architecture combined in itself both the romantic and the classic. In 1600 the Italian Marie de Medici married Henry IV, bringing with her from her native Florence the full flavour of the Italian Renaissance, to be absorbed in French culture. An early sign of this was the invention of the *Compartiment de Broderie* by the landscape architect Boyceau, of which the exhibition garden is a facsimile example. The conception, an early portent of the grandeur in garden design that was to come a few years later, is of an elaborate pattern executed in box, flowers and coloured sand. The pattern reflects the embroidery of contemporary costume, and is an indication of the highly sophisticated elegance that was to underlie the great compositions by Le Nôtre in the reign of Louis XIV. The flower was recognised only as architectural decoration.

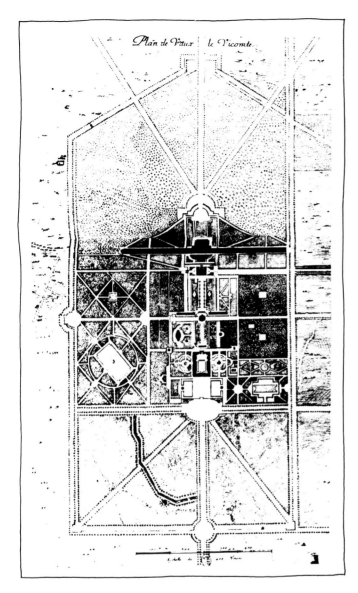

Vaux-le-Vicomte.
The first major work of André Le Nôtre

By general consent there never has been, nor is there ever likely to be, any private garden so magnificent as that of Versailles. The beginning of such a mighty conception of land space design can be traced to the layout of chateau and town of Richelieu in the Touraine (designed 1627-35 by Le Mercier as one great co-ordinated unit). Then came Vaux-le-Vicomte (above), completed 1661 for Fouquet and the first major work of Le Nôtre. The unfortunate builder, Finance Minister of Louis XIV, having roused jealousy in the monarch, was deposed and imprisoned, but his works (still considered the masterpiece of the designer) inspired the many great layouts round Paris, and most of all, the palace of Versailles. The scale of the latter was prodigious, forty thousand soldiers, for instance, being employed to bring water by canal from the country. Whole schools of art were established for sculpture, fountains and the like.

France of the seventeenth and early eighteenth centuries was the climax of classical garden history, but before progressing past the Gods and the Gothic Temple to an opposite world of imagination, we must first leap a century to enjoy a post-script to classicism — that of the happily confused art of England of the nineteenth century.

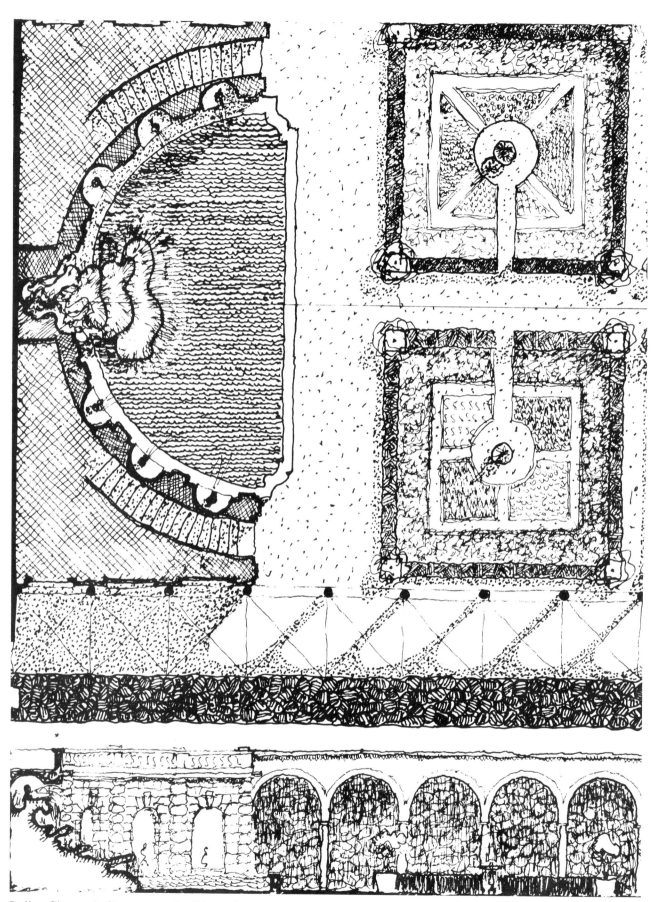

Italian Sixteenth Century — the Water God. For the metaphysical anxieties that lay below this exterior, see detail page 162

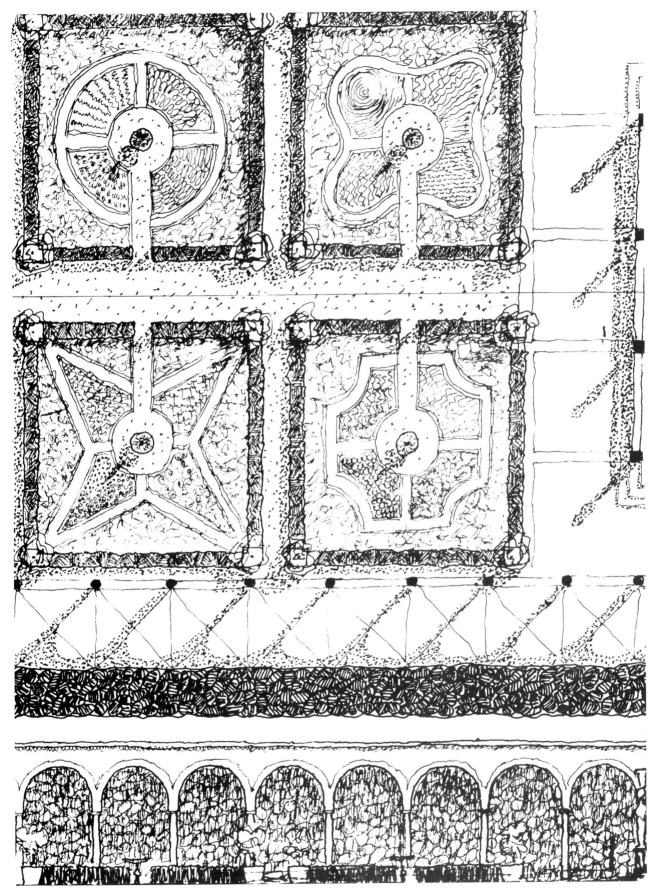

Italian Sixteenth Century — the parterre

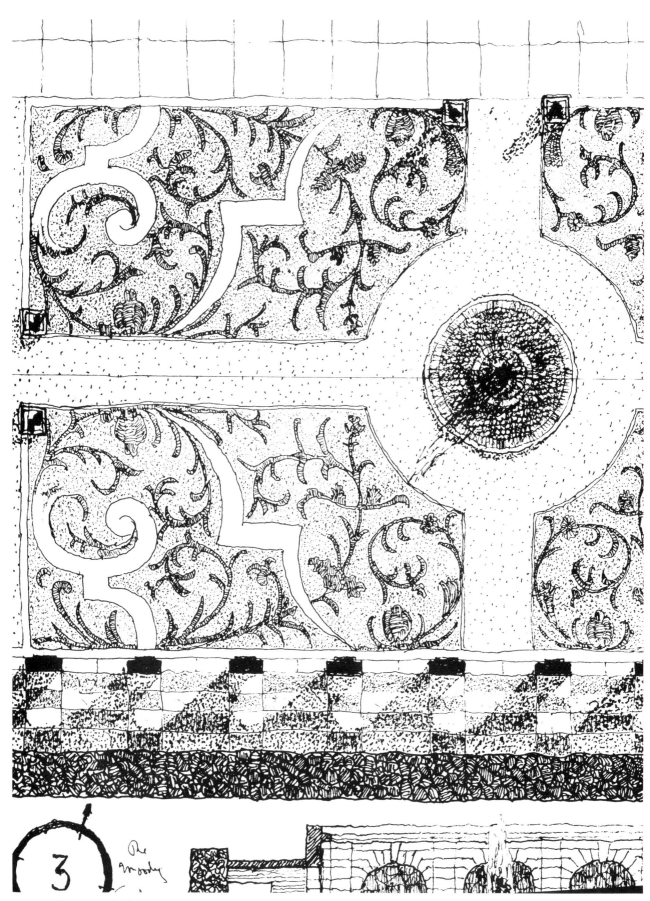

French Seventeenth Century — the parterre de broderie

French Seventeenth Century — parterre and pleached lime alleé

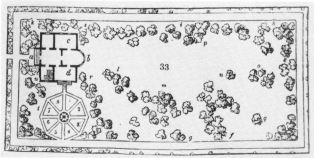

J C Loudon: the 'gardenesque' emulating the aristocratic park

J C Loudon: A 'gardenesque' folly

The Western Culture —
the English Nineteenth Century

J C Loudon: Basket decoration

ENGLAND NINETEENTH CENTURY

Prior to the nineteenth century all garden cultures, romantic as well as classical, were founded on an assured philosophy. There now enters an arguably pleasant uncertainty of what a garden should express ideologically. In mid-century Queen Victoria built Osborne, her home in the Isle of Wight off the south coast in the Italianate style, while Balmoral in Scotland was built in a style known as mediaeval Scottish Baronial. There was in fact no single domestic garden art to express the age, but rather a multitude of ideas and charming follies which taken together have certainly earned a place in garden history. Among these delights are the 'gardenesque' style of the rising middle class (above left), the neo-High Renaissance for the aristocracy, the pseudo-mediaevel for the 'nouveaux riches' — the newly rich escaping from the industrial north, the return to indigenous nature advocated by William Robinson and the eclectic garden that reflected the world-wide interests of the reign.

Three differing ideas that are still around, chosen for the exhibition garden, are shown on plan as follows: B — Bedding out of flowers made possible

Humphry Repton: Brighton Pavilion before alteration

Humphry Repton: Brighton Pavilion after alteration

The English Nineteenth Century; the Gods; the beginning of the English Eighteenth Century

through the glass house, here romanticised into a floral clock beneath a glass dome, a magnification of the one which adorned grandmother's mantelpiece (the Victorians loved conceits like this; Big Ben of the Houses of Parliament is the magnification of a grandfather clock). C — the herbaceous border invented by Gertrude Jekyll. D — the rock garden, a theoretic miniature facsimile of the mountain landscapes from which the importation of plants was made possible by Trafalgar (1805) and the consequent freedom of the seas.

In reality the nineteenth century's great contribution to landscape was not the private garden but the collective public park, derived from the eighteenth century aristocratic park and developed by Humphry Repton (opposite page) and Joseph Paxton in England, J C A Alphand in France, and ultimately F L Olmsted in the United States.

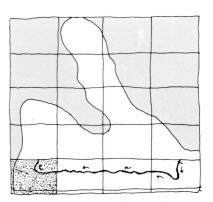

The route of the water-bus. The English Nineteenth Century; the Gods

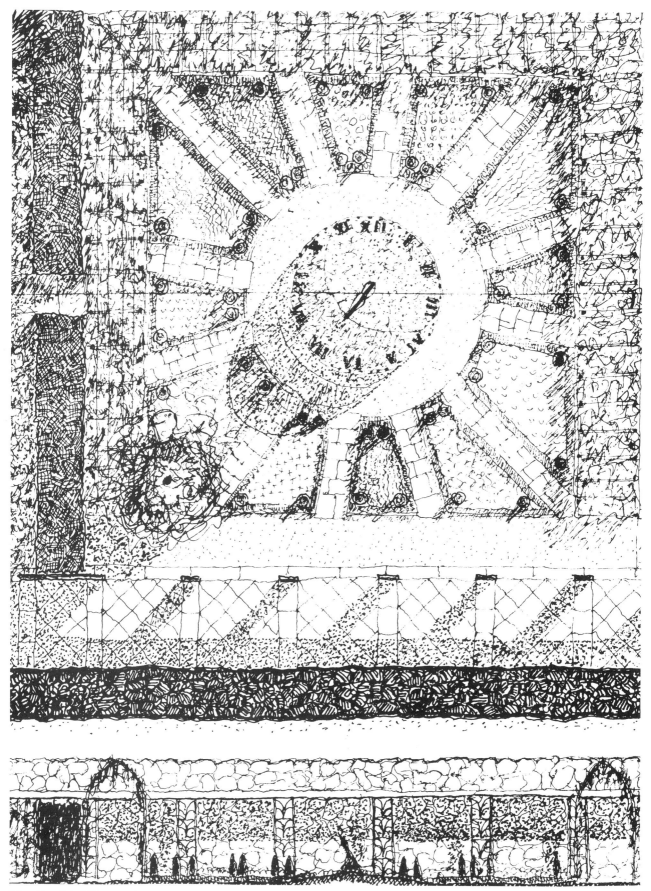

The English Nineteenth Century — Floral Clock, later altered to an Aviary

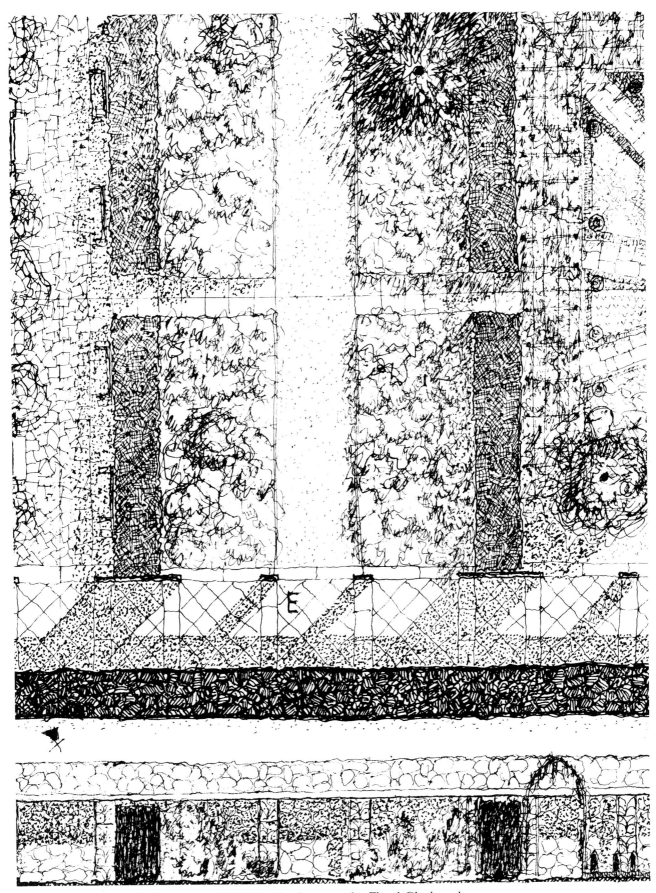

The English Nineteenth Century — Jekyll border between the Floral Clock and
Rock Garden

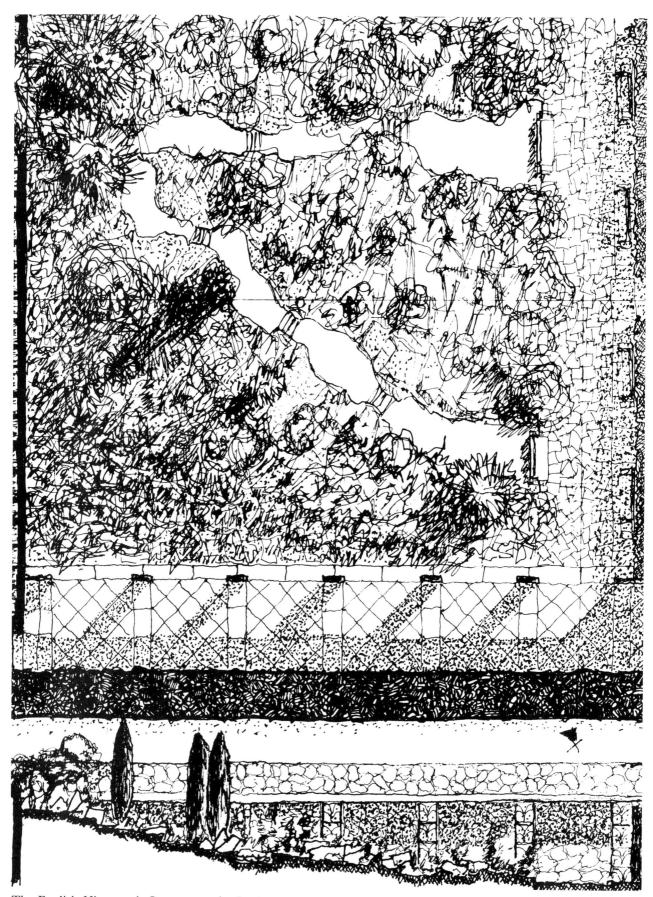

The English Nineteenth Century — the Rock Garden with metaphysical
undertones (see detail page 180)

The Western Culture —
the English Eighteenth Century

A NOTE ON SCIENCE AND ART

The transition we are experiencing from classic to romantic has deep implications for the modern world. The following is a quotation from the author's address to the joint conference of the International Federation of Landscape Architects and the American Society of Landscape Architects in Boston on 16th July 1988:

> Since recorded history the dominant art of the environment has without question been architecture. The divine gift of proportion was derived, as Plato taught, from the basic structure of the cosmos: atoms that were geometrical and rational in behaviour. Such a conception remained scientifically unchallenged until about the time that the I F L A was founded (1948), reaching a climax in painting with cubism and Mondrian, and in architecture with the international style. Then, as we have heard, things changed dramatically. No longer did science proclaim that the minutest invisible object that sustained the world was hard-edged and rational, but of a nature so extraordinary it is difficult for us to grasp. Uniting us all — we in this hall, our countryside, the planet earth, the cosmos — are invisible particles that are neither ordered nor geometric. They are undisciplined, individual and amorphous like clouds.
>
> The significance of this is that we now know scientifically what previously we only felt emotionally: that the balance of man's subconscious relation to his environment has permanently changed from hard-edged to soft.
>
> From now onwards our journey to the end will only be through 'soft' landscapes in which nature is supreme. The East has always had it so.

THE GODS

As the water-bus passes the two gods peering over the wall from outer space and their spray is on our faces, let us pause a moment and like them ruminate on what is a turning point in the relation of man and his environment. Until this time the garden had expressed only one facet of the human mind — certainly by far the most important — that of the search for order and harmony in a hostile and often chaotic world. Under the placid surface of classicism, however, were rumblings emanating from 'the strange furnishings of the subconscious mind', so described by the historian Jacquetta Hawkes. These furnishings date from pre-history, beginning with forest and savannah and from time to time exploding into the civilised world. By 1700 the modern age, the age of reason, had been born and as a counter point to this had been born, too, the age of reasoned unreason; that is to say that the unknowns of the mind were to be idealised and translated into the environment. For want of a better definition the movement was called 'Romantic', and the first to try and analyse it was the English statesman Edmund Burke in *The Origins of the Sublime and the Beautiful* in which, for instance, he traced to sex the subconscious appeal of the work of his contemporary Lancelot Brown, known as Capability, whose domain we are about to enter.

The revolution in landscape design that was to alter the course of garden history in the western hemisphere began in England at the end of the seventeenth century. Resentment against the great geometrical layouts that were fashionable after the 'Grand Tour' of Europe combined with a deep-seated love for their own countryside with its soft undulations, played havoc with the emotions of landowners. Nature's work must now predominate over man's, and Nature abhorred a straight line. Formal gardens were everywhere demolished to make way for the informal; and so were most of England's great avenues, many dating from the reign of Queen Elizabeth.

Two foreign influences stimulated indigenous thought and design. Missionaries were bringing back from China tales of a new Utopia and of gardens inspired by Nature that were sinuous, delectable and novel to the west. The new fashion, dubbed 'chinoiserie', was elegantly superficial. The second influence was that of architect and artist William Kent, who had been apprenticed to a Roman architect and had absorbed the revolutionary Baroque concept that the mind can be freed of visual boundaries and travel beyond into worlds of its own imagination. Aided by artists, poets and a gifted aristocracy, the way was now clear for the great upheaval.

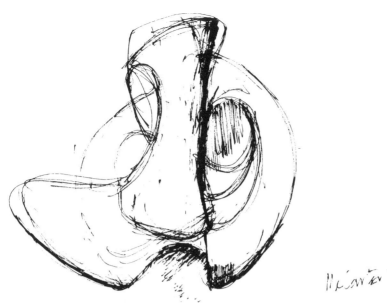

The head of Poseidon, designed by Keith McCarter

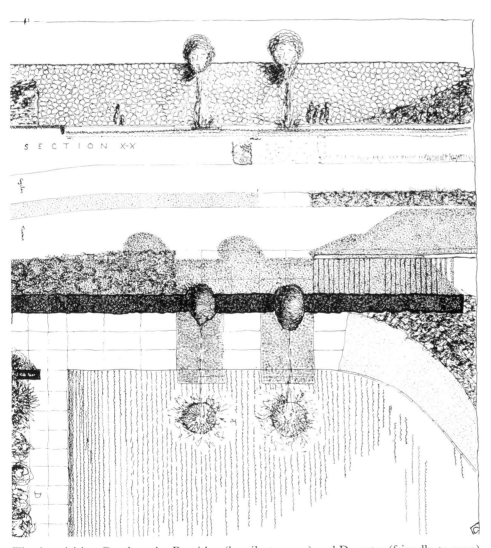

SECTION X-X

The inquisitive Greek gods: Poseidon (hostile to man) and Demeter (friendly to man)

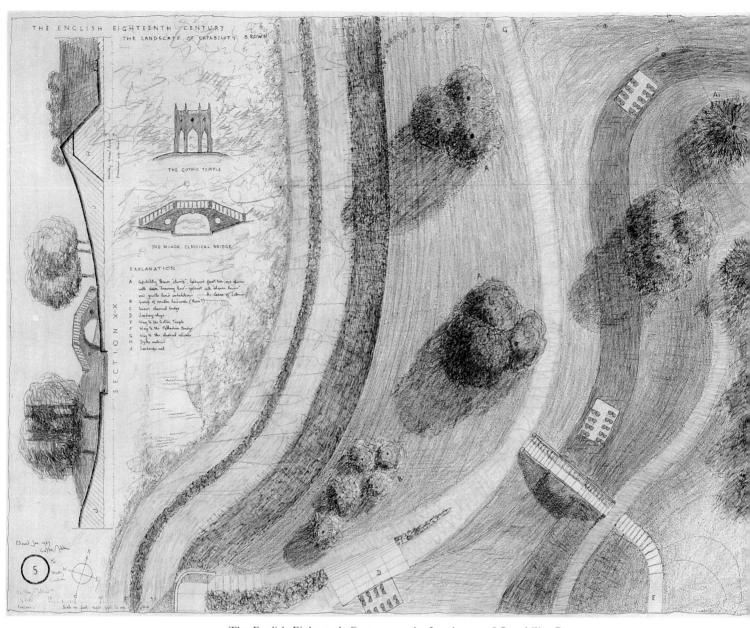

The English Eighteenth Century — the Landscape of Capability Brown

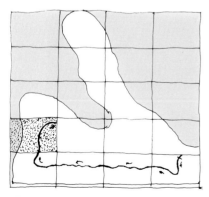

The route of the water-bus. The English Eighteenth Century

To pass from classicism into romanticism is to escape from reality into a world of illusion. The idea of a Brown park, through which we now continue, is that of a return to a mythological past where man and animal live together in a noble landscape and where there are no boundaries nor such utilities as cattle and vegetables. It is linked by architectural features to an imagined golden age, such as that of Greece, Rome or the chivalrous Middle Ages. The four basic ingredients are as follows: a) a stream would be dammed to follow the shapes of the land contours on either side, with ends concealed to suggest a mighty river; b) clumps of hardwood trees (deriving from hunting and shooting coveys) are grouped mystically on seductive undulating grass slopes that in practice would flow directly up to the Palladian mansion; c) deer are introduced to emulate idealised animals, causing a 'browsing line' to the trees;

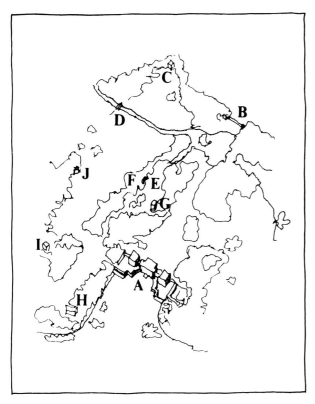

Stowe
A Mansion
B Entrance pavilion
C Temple of Friendship
D Palladian bridge
E Elysian Fields

F Temple of British Worthies
G Temple of Ancient Virtue
H Temple of Concord
I Queen's Temple
J Gothic Temple

Stowe, Buckinghamshire. Above, pictorial space as seen from the house. Below, lithograph of Stowe, 1777

and d) a sunk fence or 'ha-ha' conceals boundaries (William Kent had earlier 'leapt the fence and found that all nature was a garden').

But a Brown park is an all-male preserve and its austerity and 'shaven lawns' aroused violent opposition among those who favoured the more human and tangible style called the 'Picturesque' (below right).

The smooth lawns of Capability Brown

The same landscape conceived as the 'Picturesque'

THE LANDSCAPE OF CAPABILITY BROWN

THE GOTHIC TEMPLE

THE MINOR CLASSICAL BRIDGE

The English Eighteenth Century — the Gothic temple and the minor classical bridge

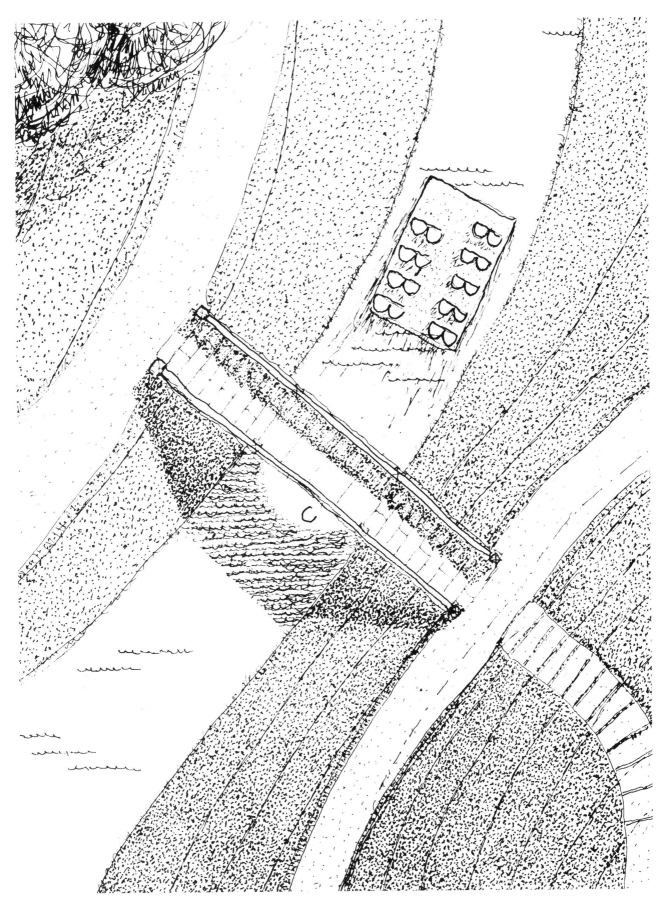

The English Eighteenth Century — the minor classical bridge and approach to the Gothic temple

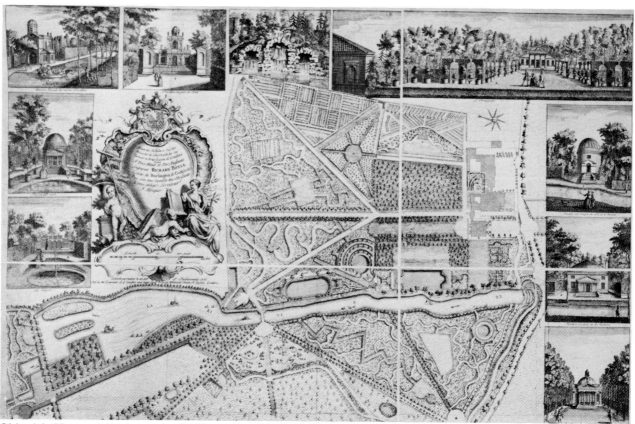

Chiswick House, Middlesex, by William Kent 1731: the transformation of the classical into the romantic

The contours planned to eliminate boundaries

56

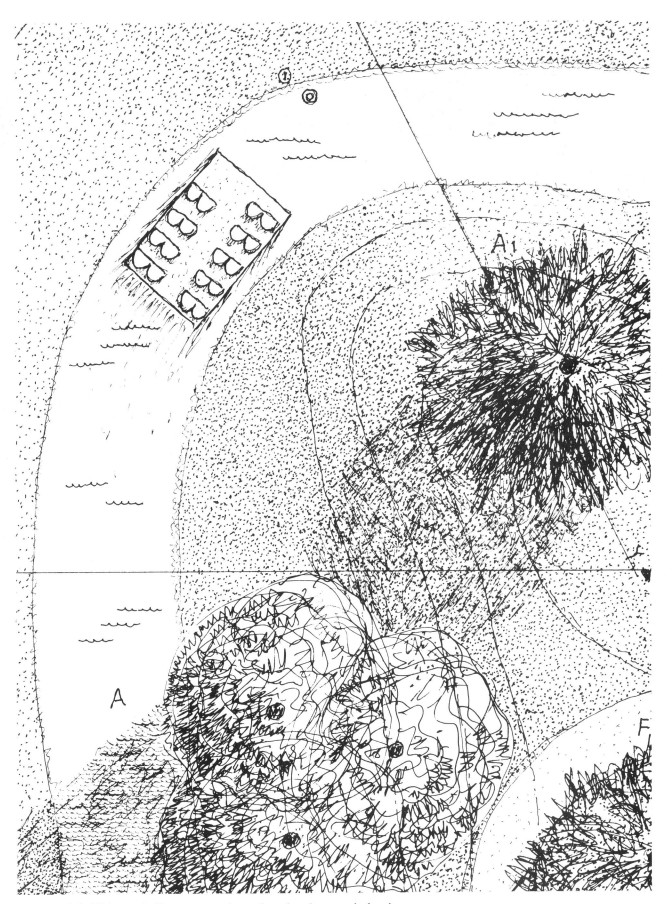

The English Eighteenth Century — viewpoints for the temple landscape

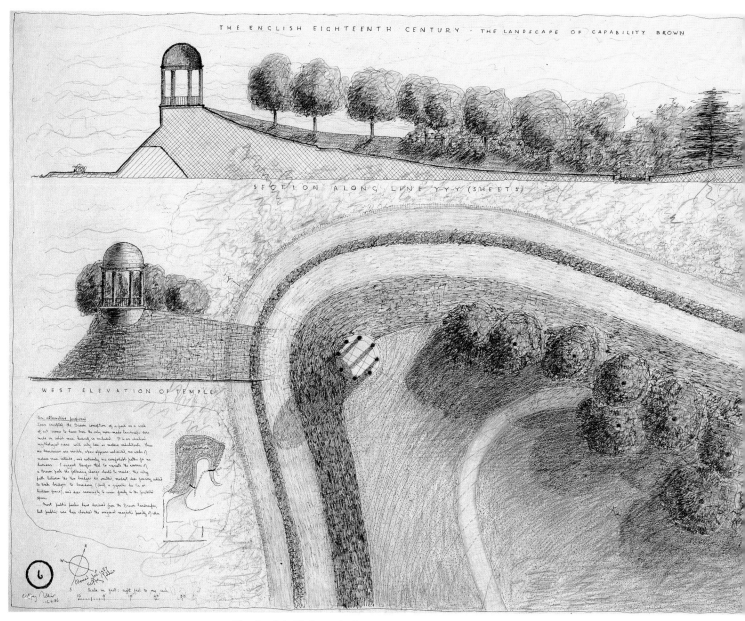

SECTION ALONG LINE Y-Y-Y (SHEET 5)

WEST ELEVATION OF TEMPLE

The English Eighteenth Century — the Landscape of Capability Brown

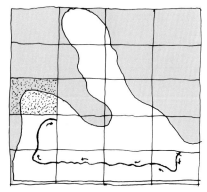

The Landscape of Capability Brown
as seen from the water-bus

The drawing illustrates the problem of incorporating a purist Brown park into a public park, for people in this mythological scenery were excluded in favour of deer. The temple was for the Gods. For this reason the public path shown will disappear in the executed design. The public will pass direct from the minor classical bridge to the Palladian bridge, and the park (seen at its best from the viewpoints on page 57) will be returned, with concealed boundaries, to deer.

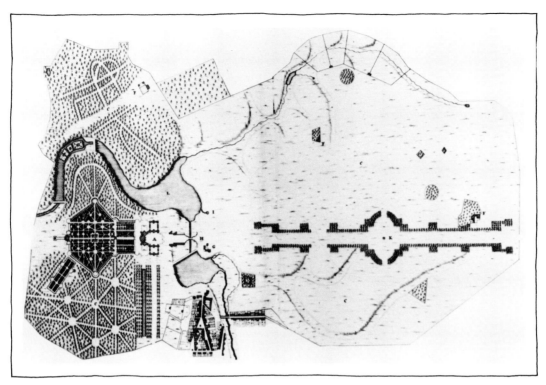

The theories of Capability Brown — Blenheim Palace before alteration

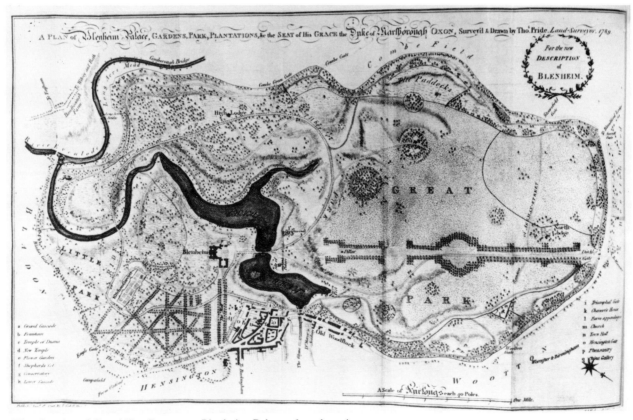

The theories of Capability Brown — Blenheim Palace after alteration

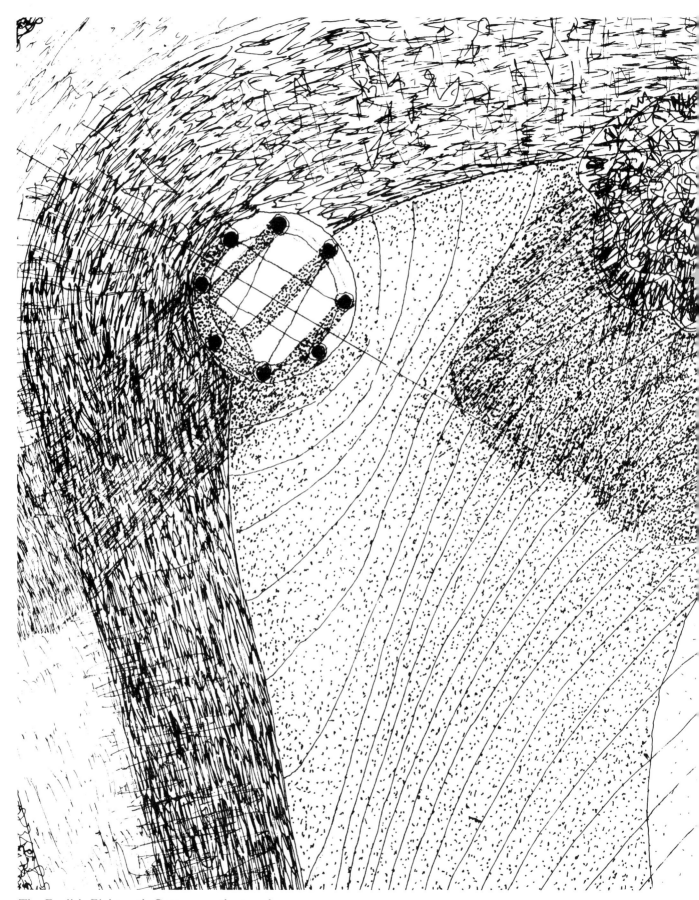

The English Eighteenth Century — the temple scenery

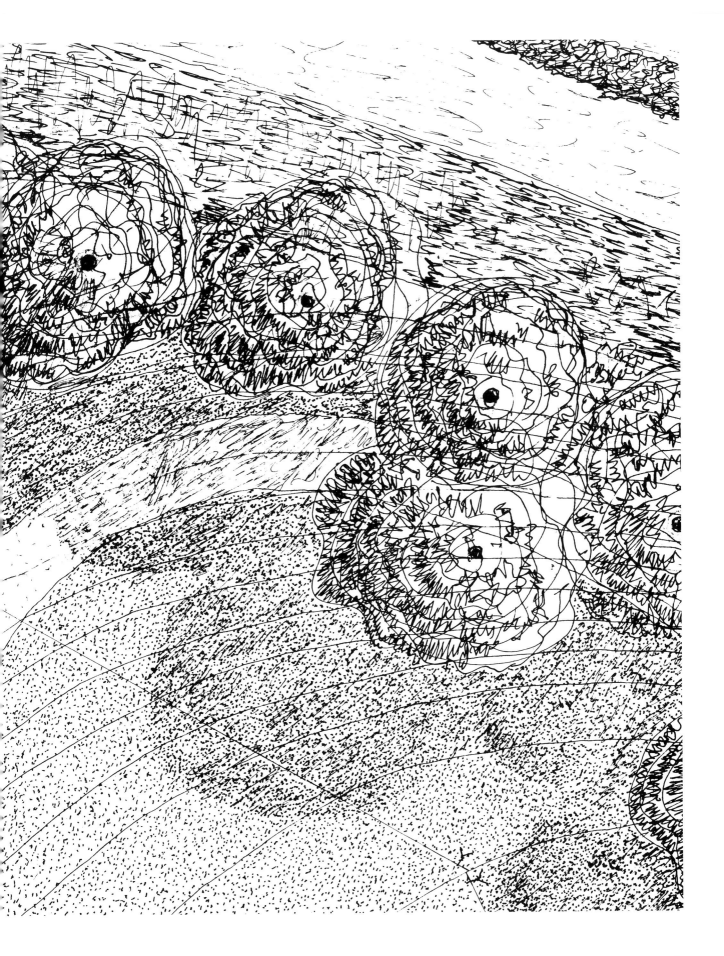

WEST ELEVATION OF TEMPLE

an alternative proposal

The English Eighteenth Century — the temple

The English Eighteenth Century — section through canal showing the water-bus
at the viewpoint on page 57

The Palladian Bridge at Wilton 1737. Designed by the 9th Earl of Pembroke and Roger Moon. (From *English Gardens and Landscape* by Christopher Hussey)

The Western Culture —
European Eighteenth Century

The voyager is now momentarily whisked away from the water-bus to climb the hill to the Gothic eye-catcher where he will see the innumerable details yet to come; the undulating Wall of China is in the distance; below him the waters of the Kent-Brown valley enriched with that most heroic of follies, the Palladian bridge; in the distance the obelisk commemorating the making of the gardens. He rejoins the water-bus, progresses through this romantic-classical

The Ruins of Roche Abbey, Yorkshire, as included in a Capability Brown landscape. The English park embraced in its ornaments the extremes of the classical and romantic

European Eighteenth Century with part of China

scenery, sweeping round the bend into the totally different and awesome valley of the Picturesque...

The Picturesque, the love and fear of nature... How universal in its appeal! What memories it provokes, both reassuring and deliberately disturbing! Why this odd urge for a throwback into the immediate and distant past?

If the subconscious origins of the simple Brownian landscape can be traced back to the savannah and man the hunter, then the Picturesque has a far more complex saga. On the one hand it seems to respond to a wish to return to the forest, the womb of mankind; and on the other to re-experience the terrors of the earliest civilisations, such as the cave and mountain perils, blood thirsty castles, a hermit or two as human freaks and what else you will in the search for dangers that from a place of safety will send a pleasing shiver down the spine.

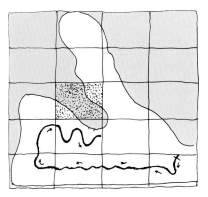

The route of the water-bus. (The details in the drawing above are included in the drawing on page 68)

E-F THE GREAT WATERF

L: THE EYE-CATCHER

European Eighteenth Century

Scale in feet:
10 0 10 20 30 40

AND THE RUINED CASTLE

B: THE PALLADIAN BRIDGE

European Eighteenth Century — the Classical-Romantic

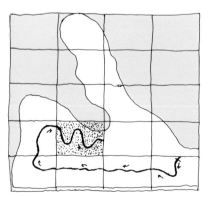

The route of the water-bus.
European Eighteenth Century

We now hear the crash and roar of water. Passing a peasant's cottage on our right and under a bridge, we find ourselves within the awesome Picturesque landscape of the kind inspired by such painters as Salvator Rosa. The scenery closes in. Gloomy conifers predominate. On the right a ruined castle looms ominously. In front the great so-called Tracey Waterfall* thunders down out of the sky from unimagined heights to ruffle the waters and splash our faces. We negotiate the hazards of the river bend, the waters calm, and we find ourselves in the very different placid landscape of France.

The France that we have entered is based on the Picturesque gardens of the Petit Trianon, made by Louis XVI in 1774-93 as an escape for the Queen from the palace of Versailles. On our left a novel and now fashionable 'chinoiserie' park with its serpentine river. Ahead is the Anglo-French hameau (hamlet) where the Queen would live the life of a peasant. The Revolution came and King and Queen were guillotined in 1793.

* Author's note: While creating the waterfall I discovered that the smiling cashier behind the desk at my Lloyds bank in Highgate, England, was unbelievably called Tracey Waterfall. A beautiful name deserving of immortality.

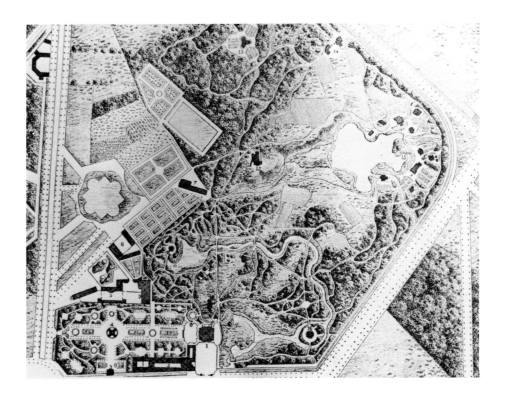

The Petit Trianon, Versailles,
showing the juxtaposition of
the Classical Gardens (1762),
the Anglo-Chinese Park (1774)
and the Anglo-English hameau
(1774-93)

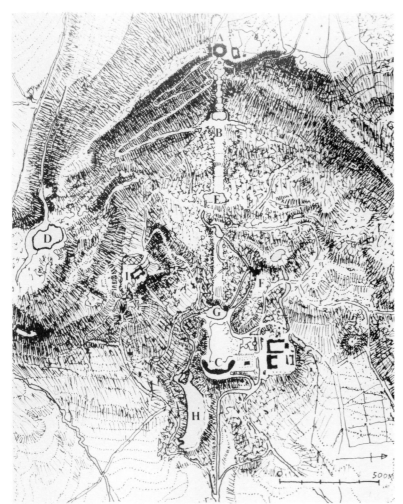

Cascade, Wilhelmsohe

The Park, Wilhelmsohe, Germany,
showing the imposition of the mid-
eighteenth century romantic landscape
upon the classical. Compare with the
Brownian plan for Blenheim page 59

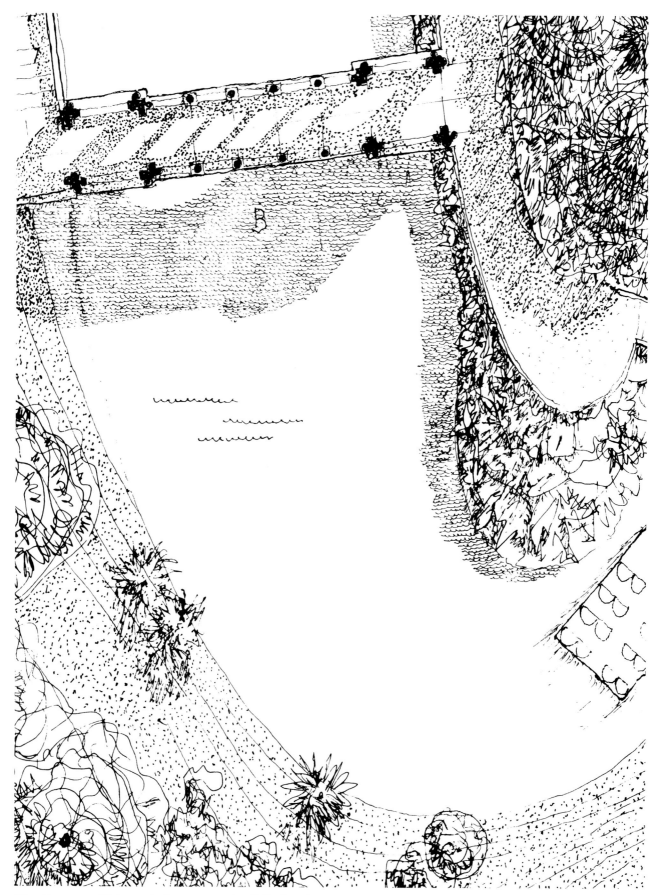

The European Eighteenth Century — the Palladian Bridge

The European Eighteenth Century — the Ruined Castle and the Tracey Waterfall

The European Eighteenth Century — the idea of the Chinoiserie park of the Petit Trianon

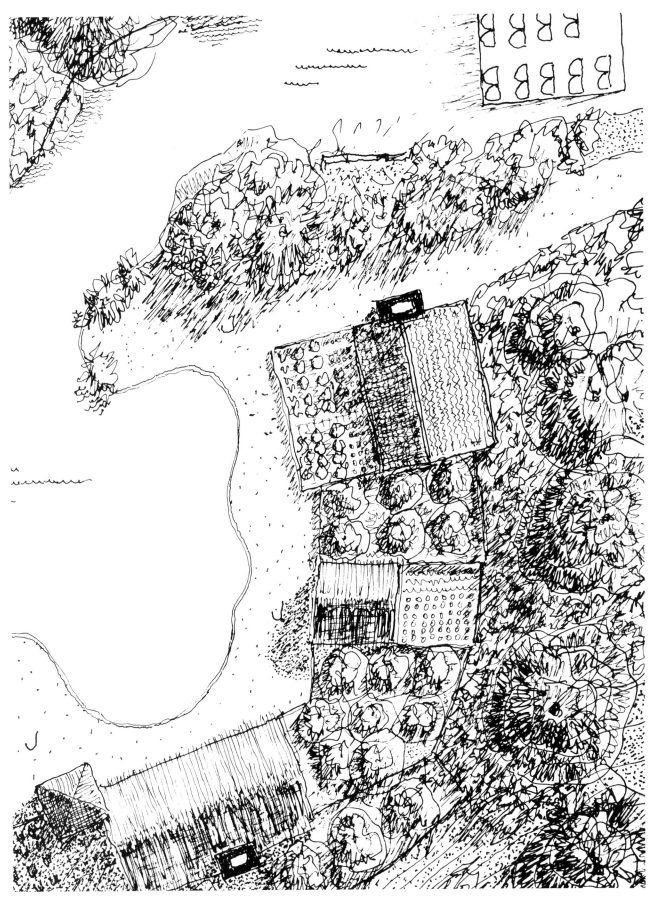

The European Eighteenth Century — the idea of the hamlet of Marie Antoinette at the Petit Trianon

Bolshoi Kapriz

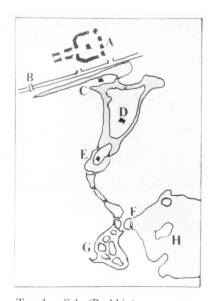

Tsarskoe Selo (Pushkin)
Plan showing Chinoiserie landscape
A Chinese hamlet
B Bolshoi Kapriz
C Creaking Pavilion
D Concert Hall (Classical)
E Turkish Kiosk
F Palladian bridge
G Archipelago
H Great lake

The Western Culture — European Eighteenth Century and the West-East Divide

Our water-bus now proceeds round a bend in the landscape with a glimpse of a hermit's grotto. Before us appears an archipelago which simulates the 'chinoiserie' in the huge eclectic park of Tsarskoe Selo (Pushkin) south of St Petersburg (Leningrad), laid out for Catherine the Great (below). We pass under a folly reminiscent of the Bolshoi Kapriz and come within sight of the great mountain divide between west and east. We pass alongside an ominous escarpment to enter an opening in the mountain side...

MOUNTAIN INTERLUDE

As if under a spell we return to the bridge leading from the campus and proceed on foot ahead through a primaeval forest. Without knowing it, we are entering the trail of a prehistoric monster that stretches from here to the sea. The forceful shape of the animal is intended to convey to the instincts of the modern traveller the horrors that once lay in the crossing of the great divide. In the recesses of the mountain we meet the plants in their natural habitat that have provisioned the man-made rock gardens of either hemisphere. Gradually plants give way to bare rock; we are on the roof of the world; we see before us the wild wet-lands and the sea beyond; and beside us that feature so dear to man since the beginning of time — the magic mountain. Let us climb this in imagination and view the lands on either side, to ponder on their difference and how this difference came about.

Let us begin at the beginning. During the Crataegus age of the reptile, about sixty million years ago, a species of insignificant insectivores appears to have sought safety from the monsters in the sub-tropical forests. These were little tree shrews, tersiers, small monkeys and apes, who peeped out from foliage, seeing without being seen. From such primates there emerged, some thirty million years later, the special family of the Hominidae, whose increasing brain and stature made them dominant in the forest and no longer afraid. Out of the Hominidae came *Homo Erectus,* a mammal which had finally lifted itself on to two feet and freed its hand eventually to use tools. Historic or present-day man is physiologically the same as this remote ancestor of over a million years ago. He is a little taller in the west, but not so in the east.

He leaves the forest to become a hunter in the open savannah. Although the immense landscapes with their groups of scrub and trees were to make an indelible impression on his subconscious, it was the animal that was his mentor. Animals were specialists and physically far beyond all-round man, but it was their collective society with its self-sacrifice of the individual to the community and its absolute standards of behaviour, order and procedure that made the deepest impression. The animal fitted the environment, but man's own attitude to this was now complex and uncertain; as hunter rather than forester he was in a new environment and appears to have sensed the existence of a world of order that lay beyond its chaotic appearance. Although he hunted the animal for food, he seems to have recognised its dignity and authoritarianism as a link between himself and the invisible world. The global

European Eighteenth Century: Russian Chinoiserie. the West-East Divide; part of Japan

impression of the age is one of animal movement within infinitely vast landscapes. Animal and place were indissolubly one, with man thrown in for good measure.

Twenty five thousand or so years ago man had spread throughout the world. The cave paintings of the west show that at that time he was still under the influence of the animals, as must have been the Chinese, whose early arts showed spiritual similarity to western cave art. Then came the parting of the ways. With a congenial geography and climate, China continued collectively and majestically along the philosopher's route of reverence for nature. Western man, on the other hand, broke tradition about 8000 BC, determined in a hostile world to be the master rather than the child of nature, eventually to free the individual from the collective and open the minds of all to unforeseeable powers.

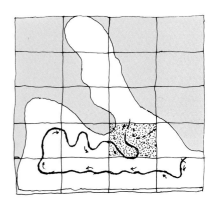

The route of the water-bus and the return. Russian Chinoiserie; the West-East Divide; part of Japan

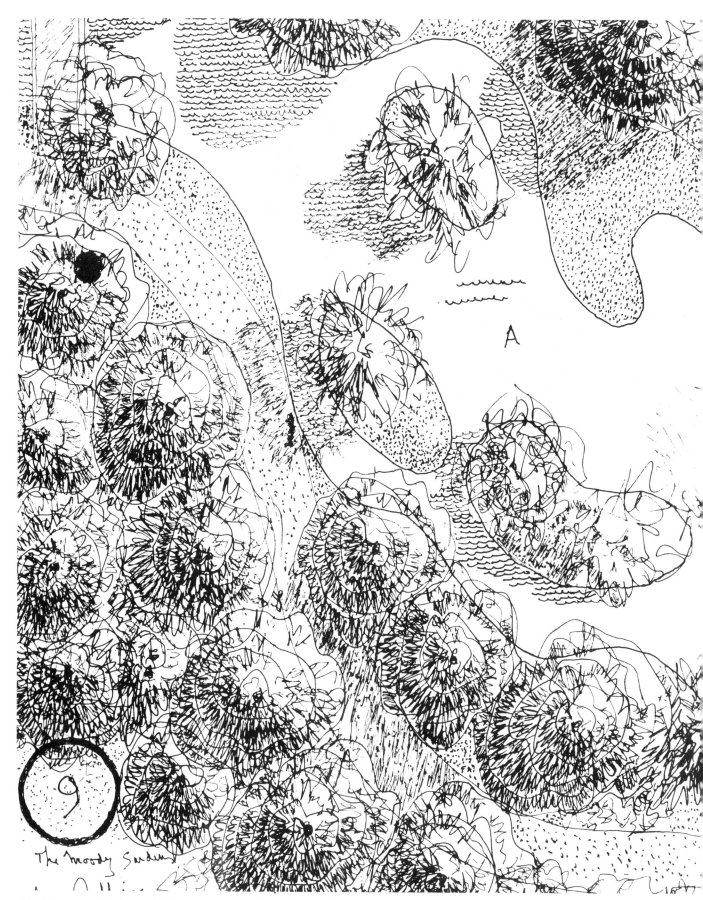

The European Eighteenth Century — Russian Chinoiserie based on an
archipelago and Bolshoi Kapriz, Tsarskoe Selo

76

A

The West-East Divide — the Magic Mountain

The West-East Divide

The Bull from the great oval cavern of Lascaux, the largest of the paintings (18 x 32in.). On the left is a red cow followed by its calf (from *The Lascaux Cave Paintings* by Fernand Windels)

Within the Mountain Divide: the First Landscape of Man

The Sagrada Familia Church, Barcelona. Designed 1900 by Gardi, showing the influence of the peaks of Montserrat

Although our water-bus passes through the mountain divide, it does not stop. To explore this underworld we must start afresh on foot from the campus. The way leads through the primaeval forest and the valley of the wild flowers to the magic pinnacles, offspring of the invisible mountain itself.

We pass through the mountain range and into the underworld. We should do well to pause and take coffee in the first cavern, for we are about to board a ferry and (unlike Charon across the silent Styx) cross hazardous waters to discover in the awesome depths ahead something beyond belief. Forget the bookstall for the time being. Enter the torchlit painted caves of Lascaux relaxed and bereft of knowledge, and you will respond to the psyche of animals and recognise the breath of human spirit within it; and feel tremendous.

The context of this beautiful man-made landscape is recorded in *The Landscape of Man:*

Between 50,000 and 8,000 BC man appears to have spread over a greater part of the globe, and was probably most populous in Africa and south-

Mystical peaks of Montserrat near Barcelona

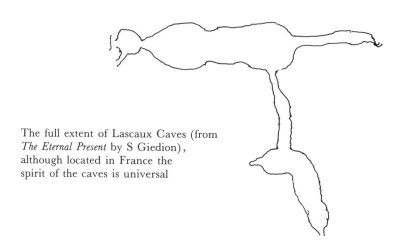

The full extent of Lascaux Caves (from *The Eternal Present* by S Giedion), although located in France the spirit of the caves is universal

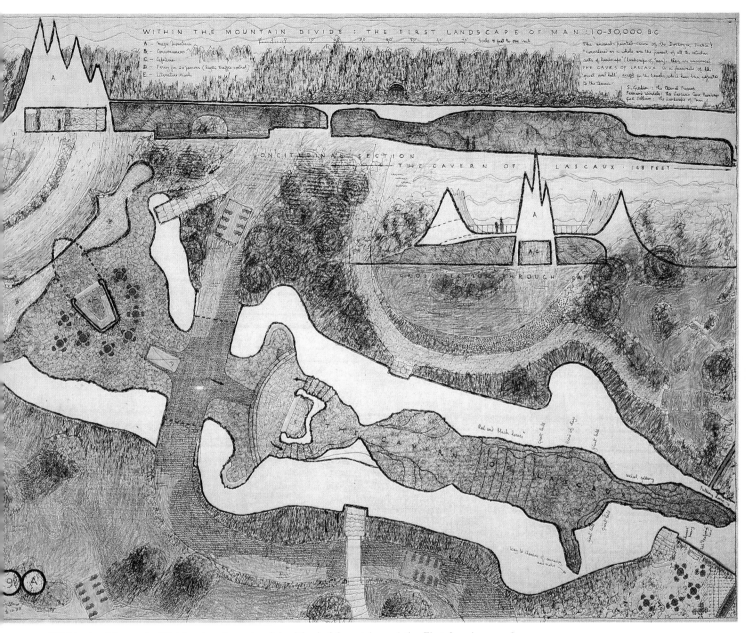

Within the Mountain Divide: the pinnacle of the Magic Mountain and the First Landscape of Man

west Asia. Where he settled he became conditioned by geography and climate into the present races of mankind: negroid, caucasoid, mongoloid, bushman and Polynesian. The caucasoid gave rise to the Central and Western civilisations, the mongoloid to the Eastern, including the Pre-Columbian American. The concept of mysterious forces behind all life was now almost universal, expressed in the worship of a Mother Goddess of fertility. The climax of instinctive man, as he may be called, is experienced in the cave arts of France and Spain. Here is an internal landscape art inspired only by observable happenings and direct experience; the mathematics and rhythms of the heavens that later meant so much to civilization, meant nothing; there was no geometry, right angle or vertical straight line. It is pure biological art that can never be truthfully repeated, the junction between *Homo erectus* and *Homo sapiens* himself.

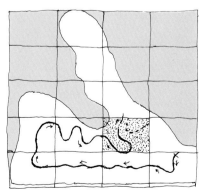

The route of the water-bus. Within the Mountain Divide. Visitors by boat are not allowed to land

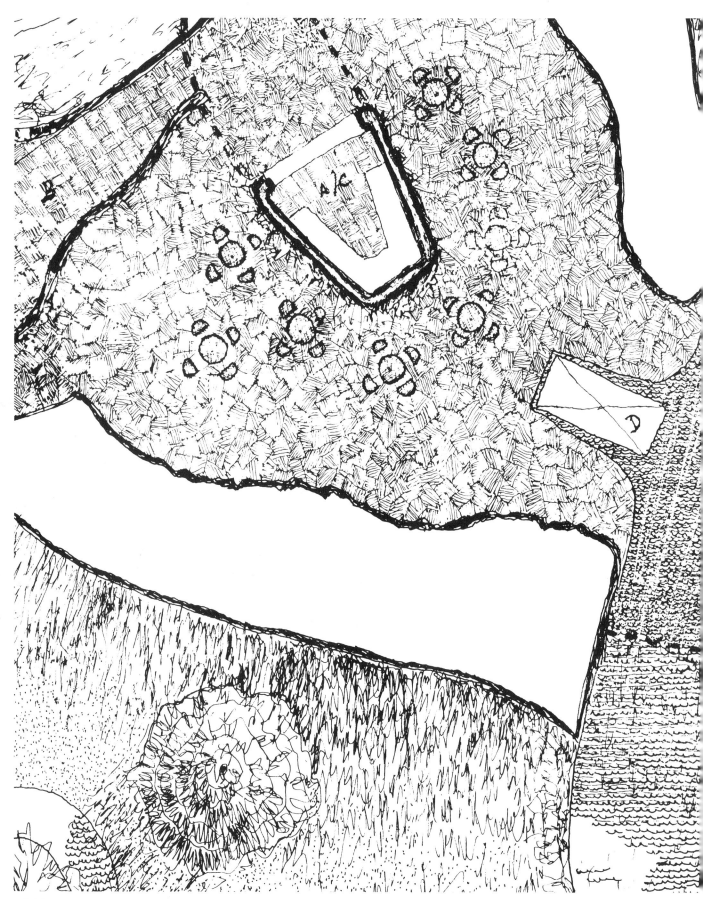

Within the Mountain Divide — the subterranean services, the ferry, and the entrance
to the gallery of Lascaux

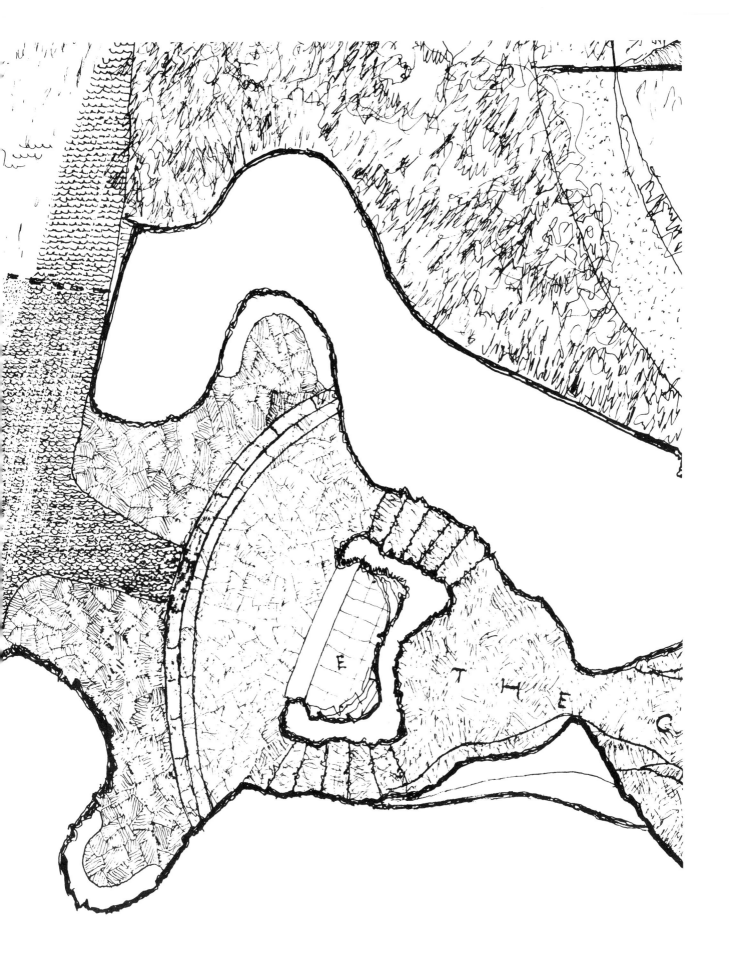

83

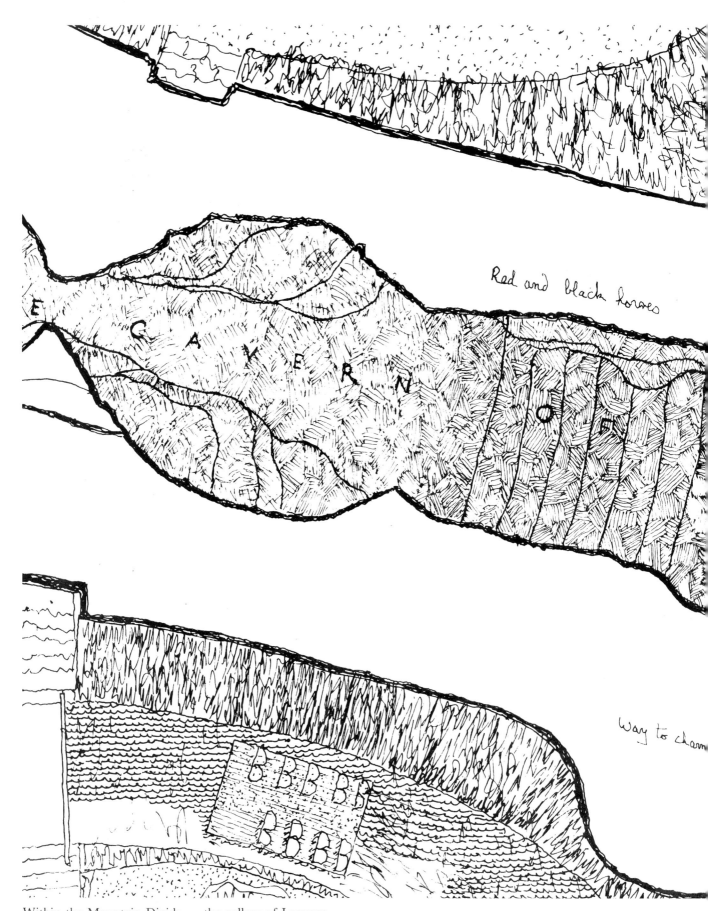

Red and black horses

Way to cham

Within the Mountain Divide — the gallery of Lascaux

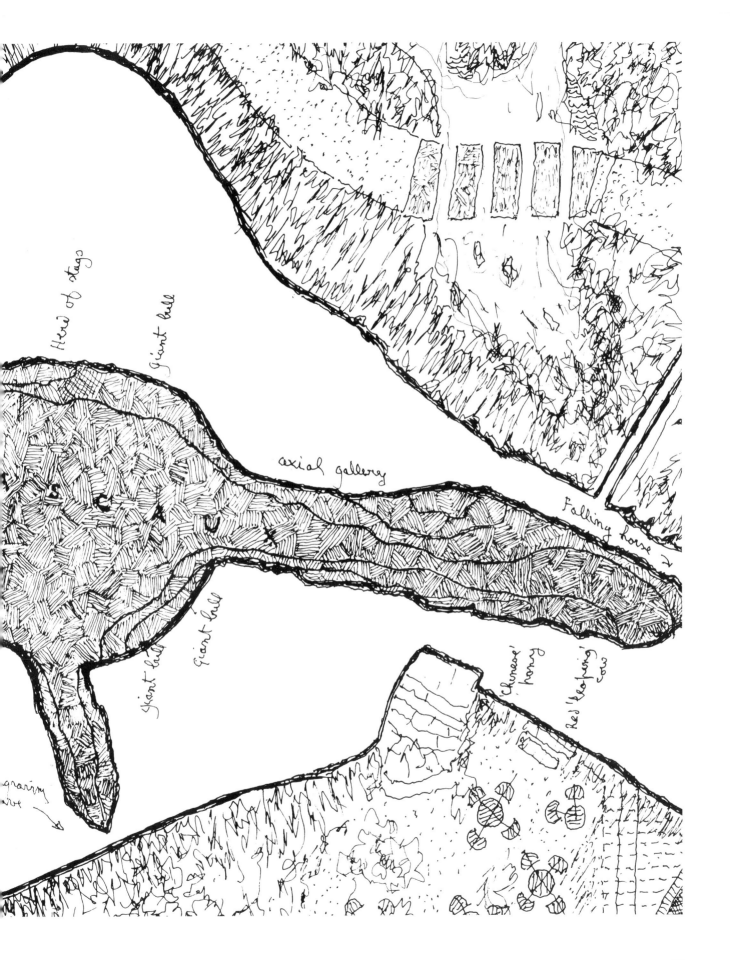

Head of stags

Giant bull

axial gallery

Falling horse

Giant bull

Giant bull

'Chinese' horse

Red 'leaping' cow

graving
...

S
C
A
U
X

The Eastern Culture — the Approach to China

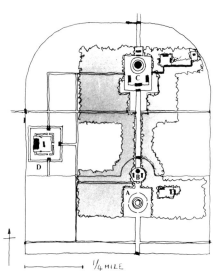

The Altar of Heaven, Peking
A Altar of Heaven
B Imperial Loft Throne
C Temple of Heaven
D Palace of Fasting

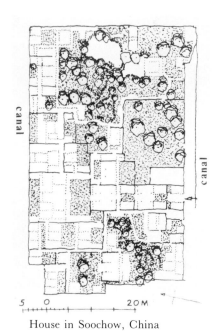

House in Soochow, China

We emerge from the darkness. The river is deeply set among cliffs and trees. 'The water seems to have changed. It has not. It is we who have changed'. What does this mean? In order to enter into the spirit of the China we are visiting, the westerner should first try to change his inherited attitude to the world about him. Normally he most enjoys water when it is decorative: the fountain fragmented to sparkle like diamonds, the foaming cascade, crystal clear water in pools and rivers. The Chinaman of our choice will have none of this. He regards water as he regards himself, a substance with a serious sense of nature, and the muddier a river the more fruitful it is and therefore the more congenial. This is the secret of Tao-ism, the mystical cult we are about to experience.

Of the two basic philosophies in China, Confucianism and Tao-ism, the former stood for a collective society designed to support central government, expressed in the sense of power of the great symmetrical buildings of the various Emperors. The opposing philosophy of Tao-ism, deriving from the metaphysician Lao-Tse and later merged into Buddhism (page 92) was the religion of the merchant class families who remained constant under their successive conquerors, barbarian and otherwise. It taught that man was an individual, part of the cycle of nature and, together with nature, was absorbed into the cosmic forces. All art was symbolic. The human body itself, for instance, reflected the structure of the world. *Rocks* symbolised the bones of this structure (the *Yang,* the stimulating male force), while *Water* symbolised the flows within the structure (the *Yen,* the tranquillising female force). Plants were of less significance, being ephemeral and loved for their passing elegance, like costumes.

Confucianism is static, whereas Tao-ism points the way to an unknown destination, the art being one of movement. The art is not a mirror to nature but rather a realisation of ideas that lurk in the subconscious, far deeper than the single idea of the cosmos itself. Tao-ists hold that these ethereal ideas are the projection of the *real* world of the subconscious into the *unreal* world of the conscious. How can this intensely personal feeling be conveyed to voyagers from another hemisphere who come collectively and briefly to invade the domain of the solitary, the contemplative and indeed the sacred? It cannot; but just as a change of attitude to landscape may already have taken place, so an illusory environment may by suggestion reveal the delicacy, beauty and grandeur of the subconscious. But only the imagination can create the spirit that flows through and unites all things.

THE WAY

'In your fancy you enter a painting', said Yuan Yen in the sixteenth century, and this is precisely what we are about to do. Our own painting is a distillation of two thousand years of Chinese landscape art. It becomes a theatre in which we ourselves have a part to play, moderns though we are. The scenery is academically correct in detail, but innovative in time and space in the assembly of the parts. The white walls are space divisions rather than enclosures. The composition is symbolic of the movement of civilisation towards an unknown destiny. Three scenes follow one another in sequence. The first scene is Tao-ist, the second Tao-Buddhist, and the third Buddha.

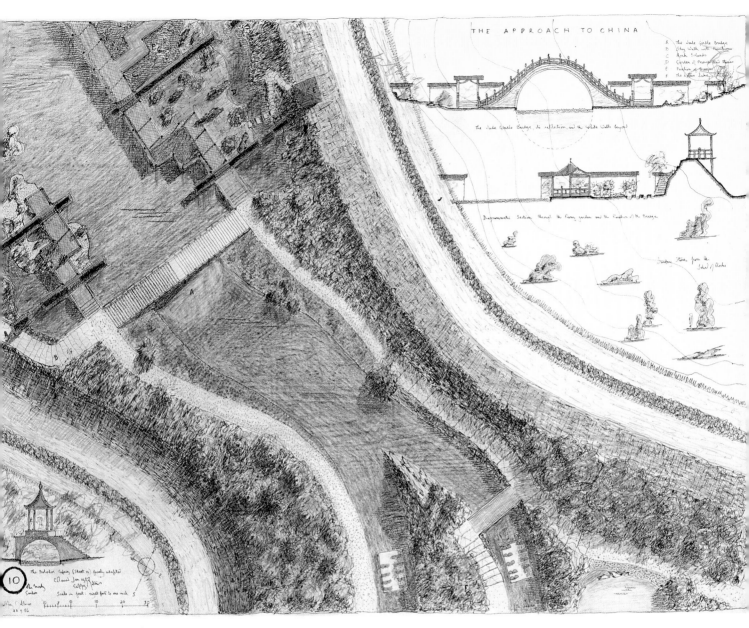

The Approach to China

We proceed. On the right is a sharp pinnacled rock that divides the outward route from the return. Round the bend we confront the entrance to China, the Jade Girdle Moon Bridge reflected in the water to form a perfect circle, the symbol of harmony. On the left a stairway leads to the viewing terrace that serpentines along the mountains like the Great Wall (the Islands of the Immortals that appear and disappear in the far distance are not at home today). We pass under the bridge. Ahead stretch the covered ways, zig-zagged to confuse evil spirits. On our left the Island of Symbolic Stones, whose strange forms and groupings are those of a human family; found in the mountains they satisfy our Chinaman that if he cannot retire to the solitary mountain hut, the mountains and their mystique must come to him. On our right, a garden of flowers and fragrance, closed within white walls on either side but open to the stream, the wild flowered hillside, and the Pavilion of the Breezes on the mountain top. On beyond, a peony garden.

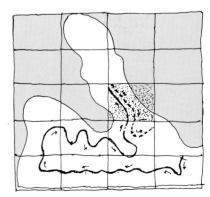

The route of the water-bus and the return. The Approach to China

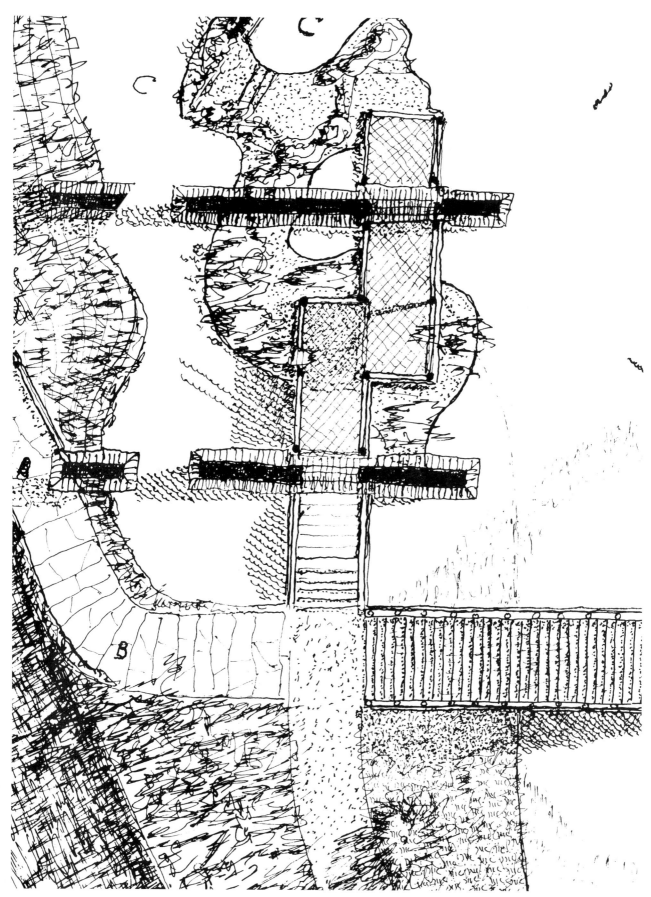

The Approach to China through the Jade Girdle bridge. On the left the island of symbolic stones. On the right a peony garden

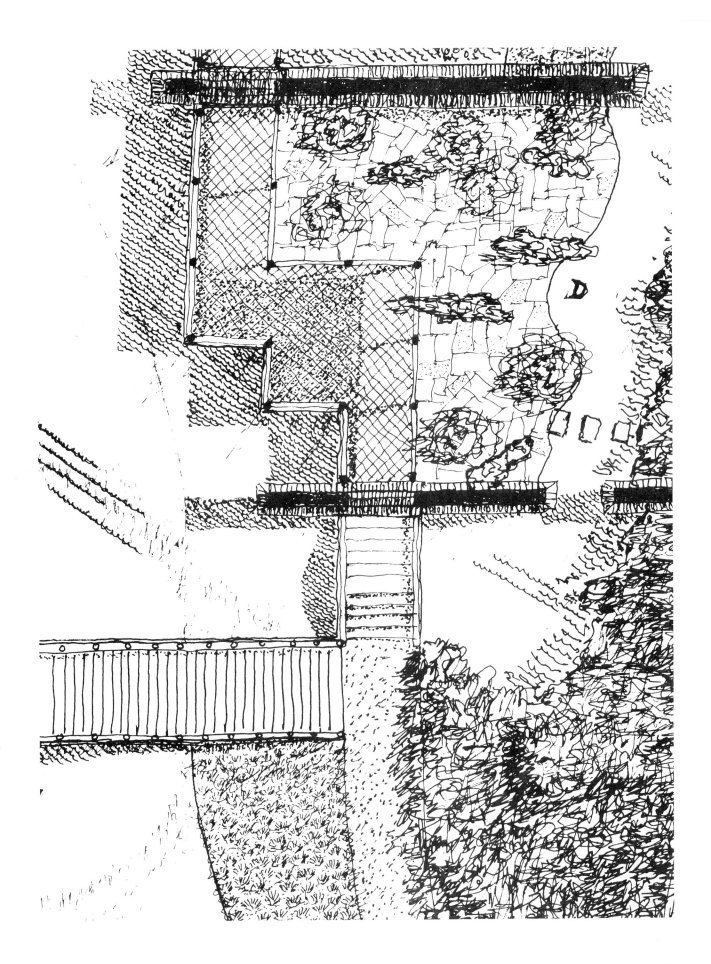

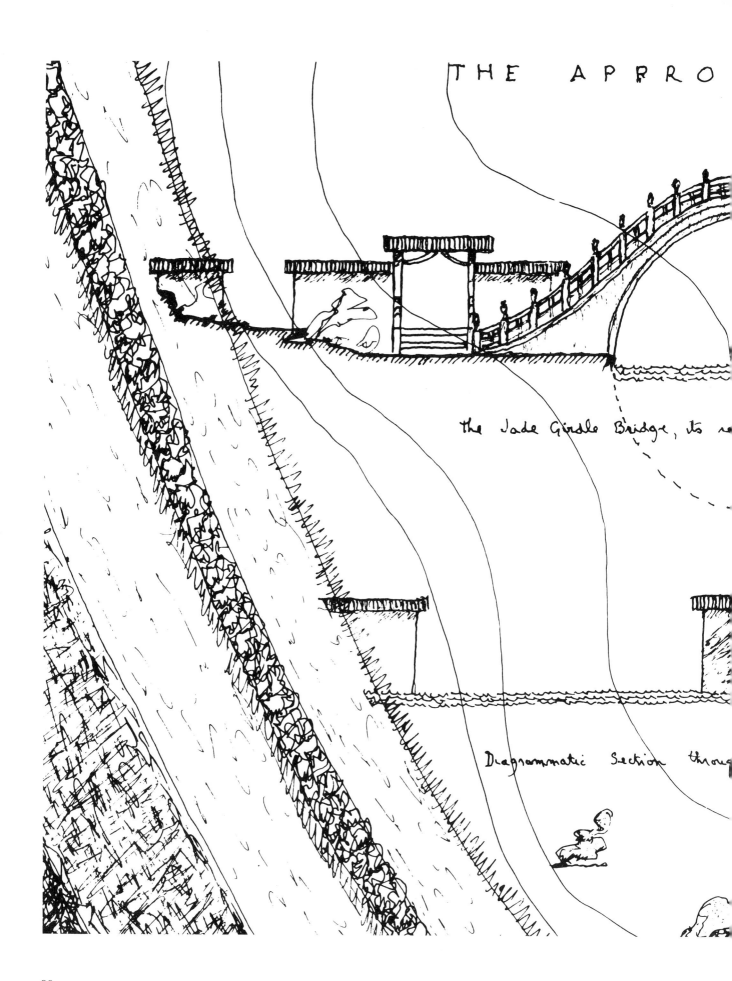

the Jade Girdle Bridge, its r

Diagrammatic Section throu

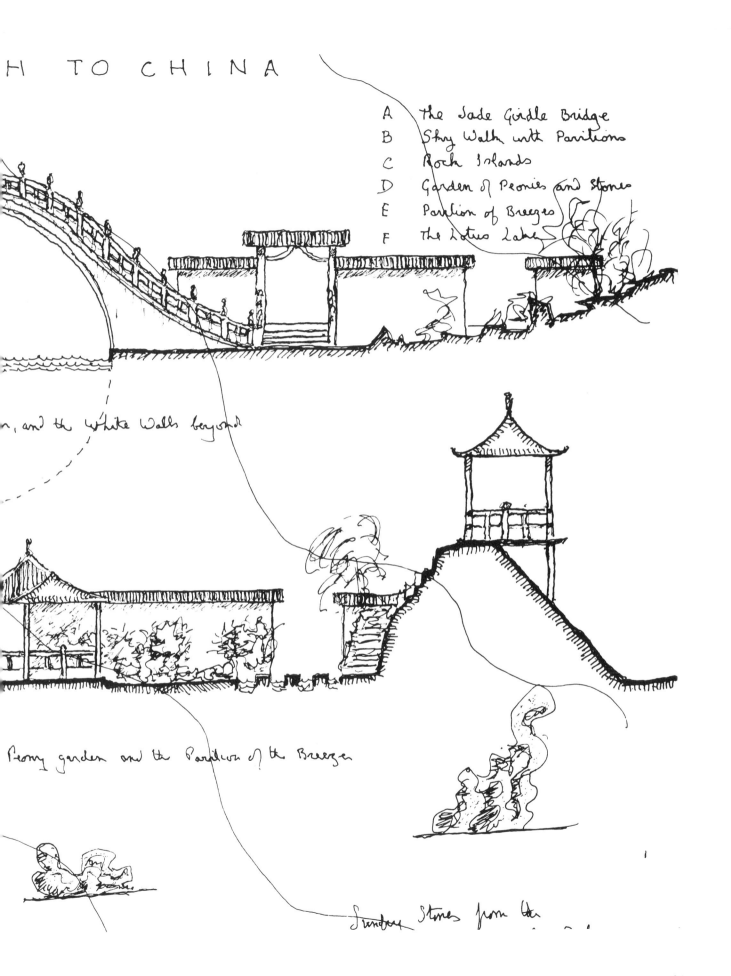

A   the Jade Girdle Bridge
B   Sky Walk with Pavilions
C   Rock Islands
D   Garden of Peonies and Stones
E   Pavilion of Breezes
F   The Lotus Lake

, and the white Walls beyond

Peony garden and the Pavilion of the Breezes

Sunday Stones from the

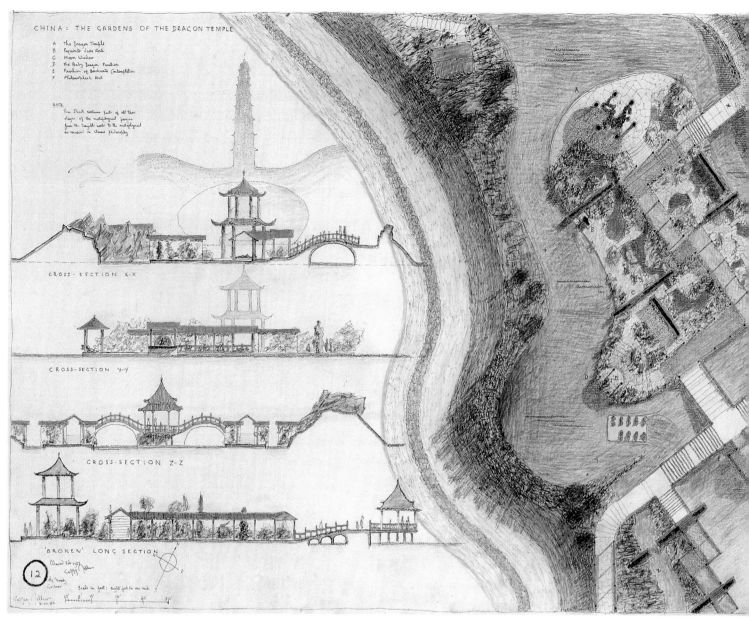

CHINA: THE GARDENS OF THE DRAGON TEMPLE

A   the Dragon Temple
B   Exquisite Jade Rock
C   Moon Window
D   the Baby Dragon Pavilion
E   Pavilion of Backward Contemplation
F   Philosopher's Hut

NOTE
This Sheet contains parts of all those
stages of the metaphysical journey
from the temple world to the metaphysical
or nowhere in Chinese philosophy

CROSS-SECTION X—X

CROSS-SECTION Y—Y

CROSS-SECTION Z—Z

'BROKEN' LONG SECTION

China: the Gardens of the Dragon Temple

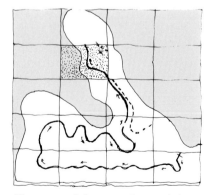

The route of the water-bus and the
return. China: the Gardens of the
Dragon Temple

The Eastern Culture — China: the Gardens of the Dragon Temple

We approach the twin bridges, between which lies the Pavilion of Music (we
are told that on summer evenings there is marvel in the lights of lanterns and
the sound of strings). We pass under a bridge and into the waters that embrace
the Island of the Celestial Bell. We swerve to the left and skirt the temple of
a little dragon. On the mountain ahead is a scholar's hut. There comes into
sight the Temple of the Dragon itself, through which are seen the mountains
that lead up to the Buddha and the Pagoda. The dragon, prostrate on the floor,
is a truly formidable character. He is the controller of waters and giver of rain.
Of him the Japanese writer Okakura Kakuzo writes: 'We associate him with

Bhaishajya, Guru, Buddha with sixteen divinities, painter unknown, fifteenth century (from Eumorfopoulos collection by Laurence Binyon)

the supreme power or that sovereign cause which pervades everything, taking new forms according to its surroundings, yet never seen in final shape. The dragon is the great mystery itself'. We enter the landscape of the Buddha.

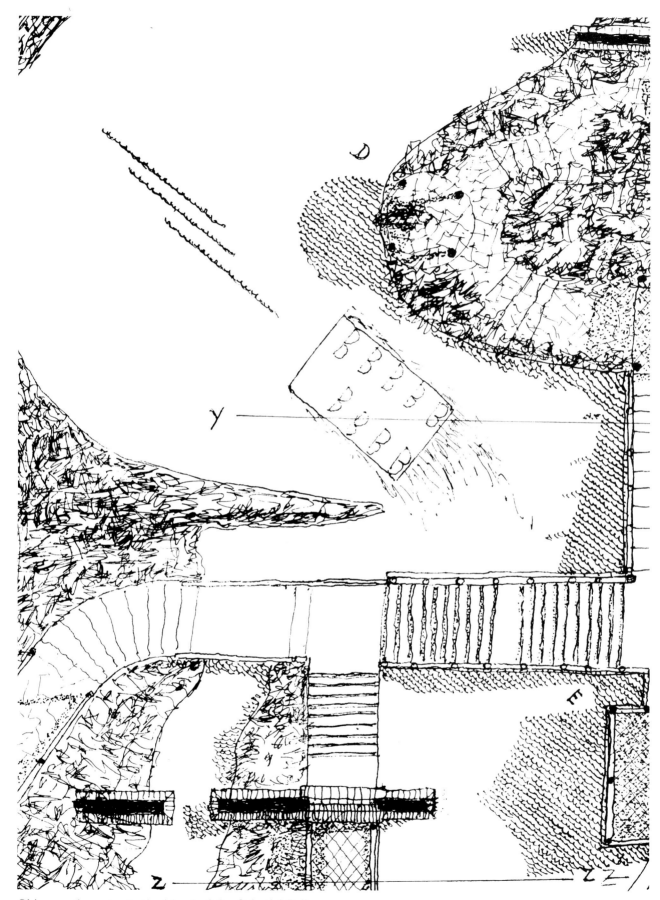

China — the entry to the island of the Celestial Bell

China — the Gardens of the Dragon Temple

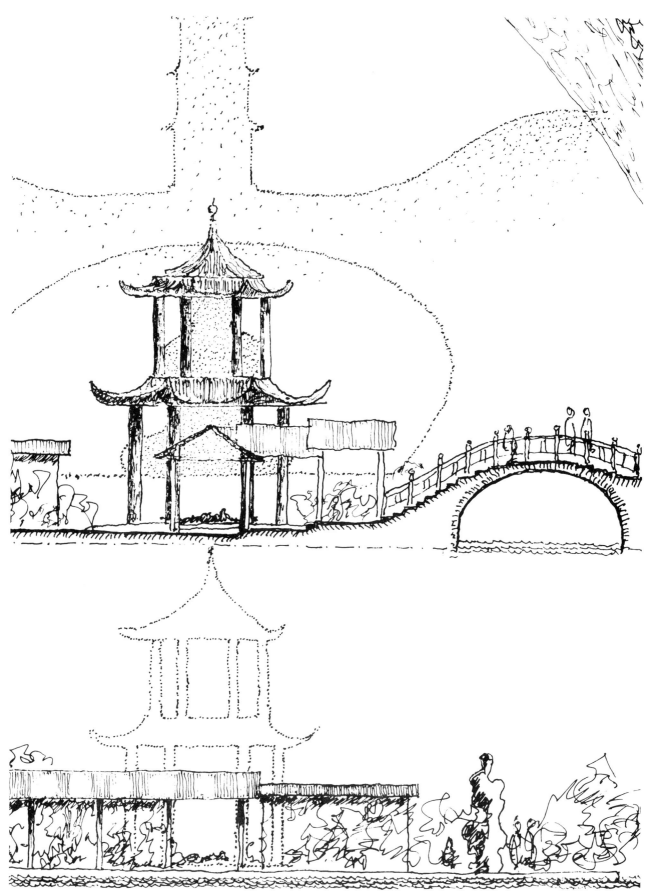

China — looking through the Dragon Temple to the distant Buddha and pagoda

SS-SECTION Y-Y

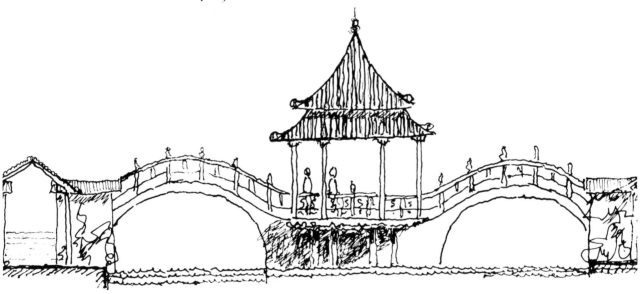

CROSS-SECTION Z-Z

China — the twin bridges and music pavilion at the entrance to the gardens of the
Island of the Celestial Bell

CTION Y-Y

CROSS-SECTION Z-Z

China continued — the Pavilion of Music and Island of the Celestial Bell

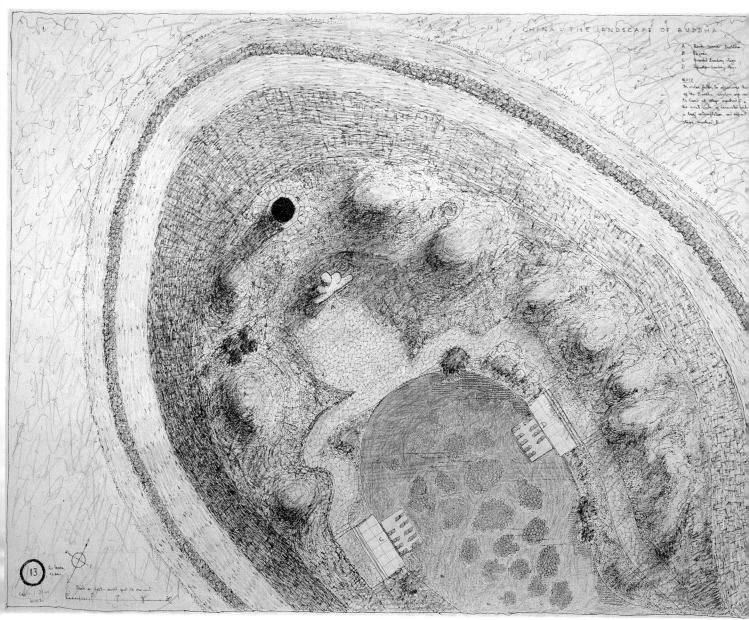

China: the Enclave of Buddha

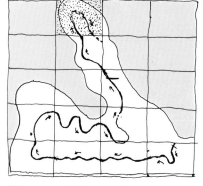

The route of the water-bus. China: disembarkation and re-embarkation at the Enclave of Buddha

The Eastern Culture — China: the Enclave of Buddha

We are now within, and part of, the deepest symbolism of Chinese philosophy, an experience unknown in western landscape art. Before us the lotus lake, the Buddha crowned with the pagoda, and the voluminous mountains from which the Buddha has emerged. The lotus lake tells the story in the words of Osvald Siren: '...it may be said to be a symbol of noble endeavour, spiritual beauty. It grows up spotless out of the mud (the material world), through the water (the emotional middle region) to the surface and the free air (the world of the spirit)

100

頸曲銀鉤雪作衣
晴川浴罷碧漣漪
正當青草人先見
行傍白蓮魚未知

Lotus and white herons. Ming period (from the Eumorfopoulos collection by Laurence Binyon)

where it unfolds its perfect perianth to the sun, thus illustrating the unfolding and flowering of the human spirit or Buddha-nature. But the full-grown flower may also stand for the pure doctrine and Buddha's throne: Buddha sits, as a rule, on the lotus flower...' Our barge passes to the left of the Lotus Water Garden. We disembark for the only time in the tour. We walk by a devious path to the grand circle of the Buddha. We meditate, and re-embark for the journey home.

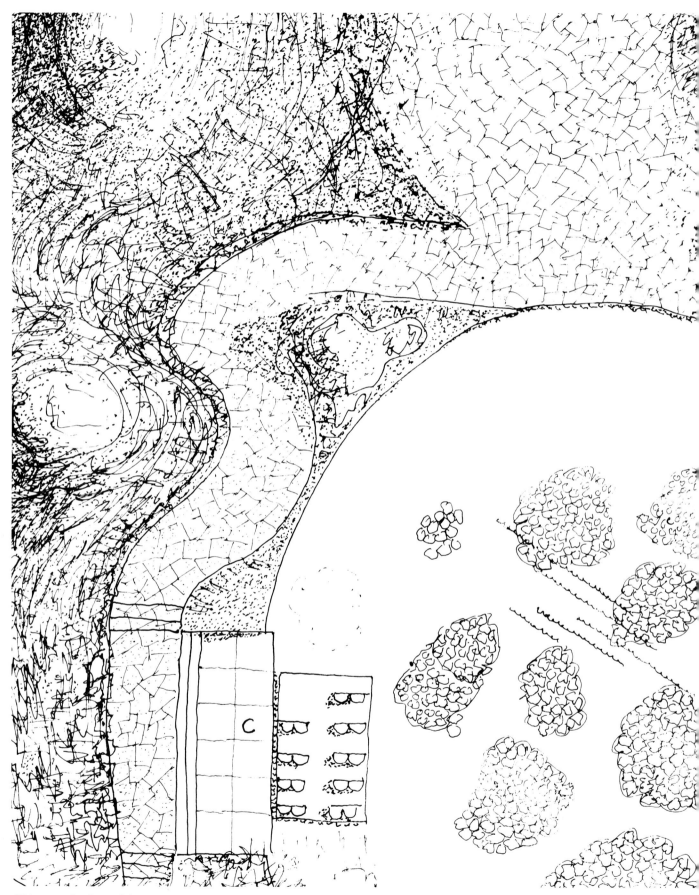

China — the lotus lake

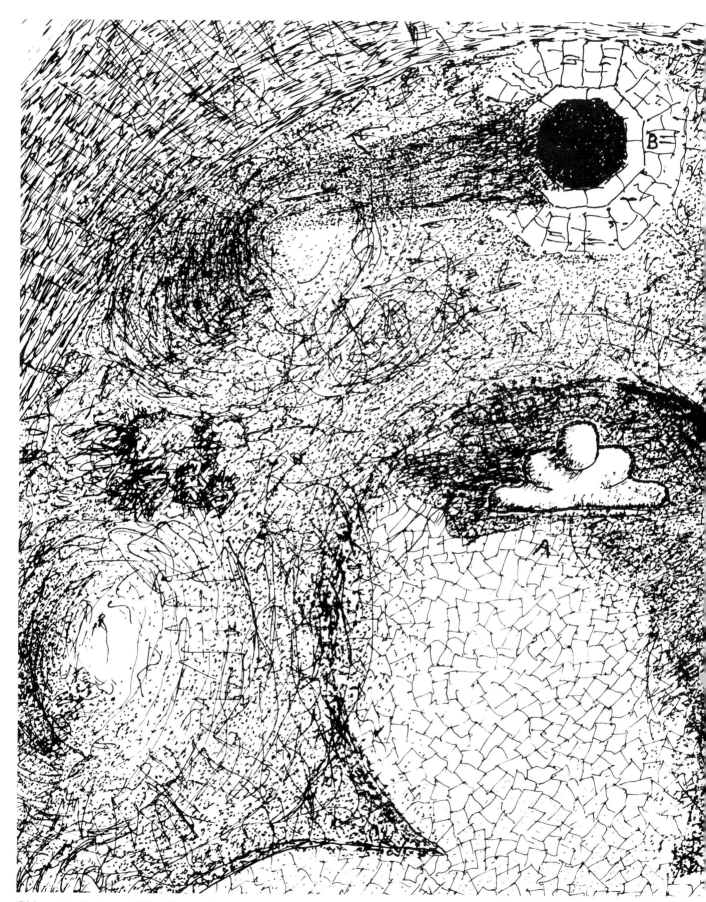

China: the Enclave of Buddha — the rock-carved Buddha with the pagoda above

China: the Gardens and Landscape of Buddha

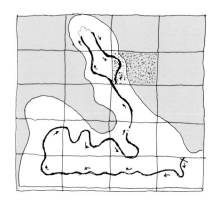

The route of the water-bus.
China: the Gardens and Landscape
of Buddha

The Eastern Culture — the Gardens and Landscape of Buddha

We pass east of the Island of the Celestial Bell; past a giant stone extricated from the mountains; under the bridge of the Pavilion of Music; past the walled gardens of peonies and chrysanthemums; under the Jade Girdle Bridge; to wake as from a dream in the waters that separate China and Japan, two widely different cultures within the enfolding Buddha.

Boating by moonlight attributed to
Ma Yüan, thirteenth century (from
Eumorfopoulos collection by
Laurence Binyon)

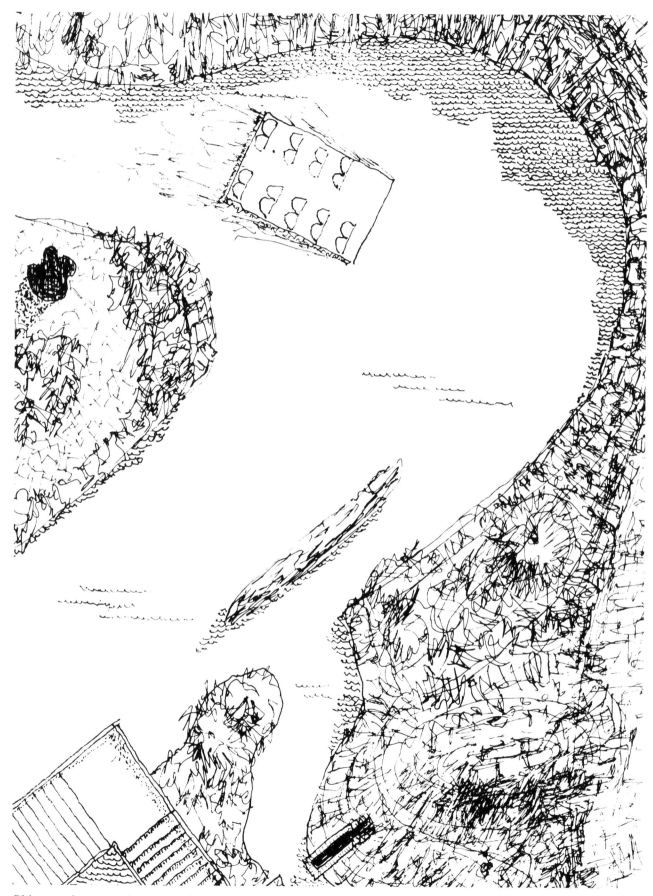

China — the return journey to Japan

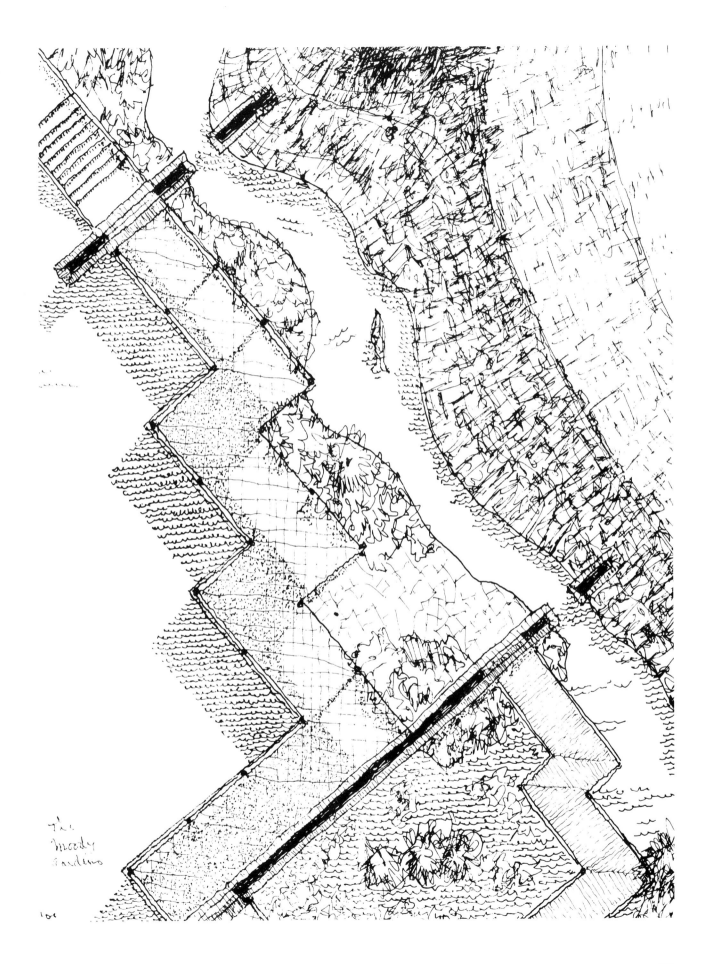

The
Moody
Gardens

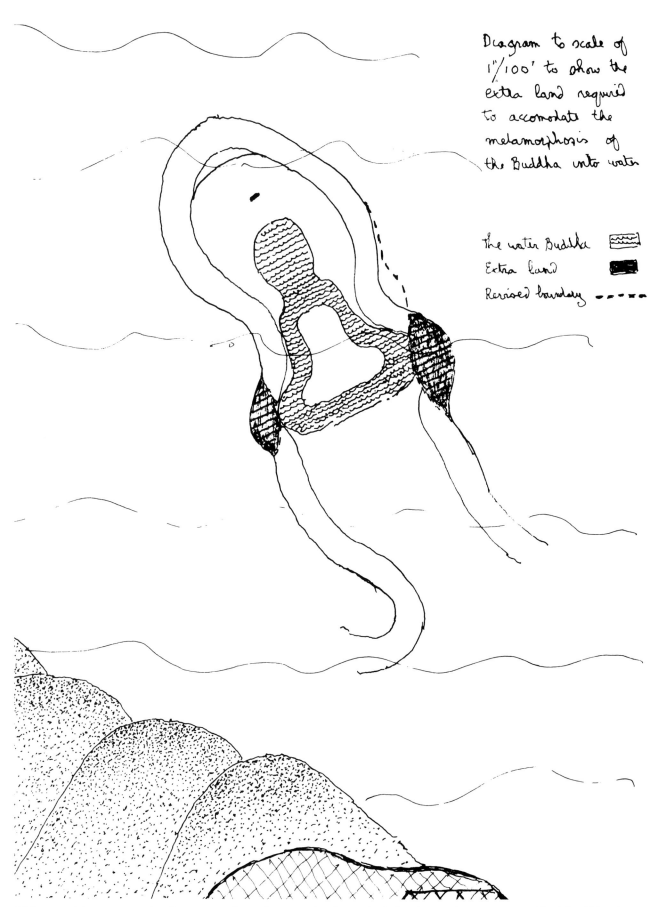

Diagram to scale of
1"/100' to show the
extra land required
to accommodate the
metamorphosis of
the Buddha into water

the water Buddha
Extra land
Revised boundary

China — this true-to-scale diagram to show the extra land required for the project metamorphised itself in the dream of immortality and flight of the soul as depicted in a sixteenth century painting (*Landscape of Man*, page 72)

China — this cross-section has since been adjusted to suggest that Buddha and rock are synonymous

An Emperor in exile AD901, artist unknown (from *Japan,* by Bradley Smith)

The Eastern Culture — Part of Japan; the Primaeval Forest

JAPAN

'On islands where the immensity of sea and sky was dominant, the basic Japanese religion, Shinto, has been concerned with the elements of the universe as a whole. The primitive Japanese worshipped the sun, the moon, the sea, the earth, the mountains, wells, springs, stones and rocks, the deities of thunder, wind, rainstorm and fire; and those of the terrifying earthquake. He worshipped the serpent and other animals, and, in due time, the Emperor himself' (*The Landscape of Man*). We pass the rock pinnacle and enter a landscape that is small in scale and rich with the sights and sounds of nature. A waterfall is heard. Our transport is unorthodox, for there are no navigable rivers in Japan; lakes turn in upon themselves. Of the multitude of garden ideas inspired as microcosms of nature we shall glimpse three from Kyoto.

The 'borrowed' landscape (page 75) is derived from the Golden Pavilion, 1394. In a compressed natural landscape there developed an urge to extend the sense of space either outwards or inwards. From the pavilion that seems to float above the water the eye passes across the symbolic tortoise island and through

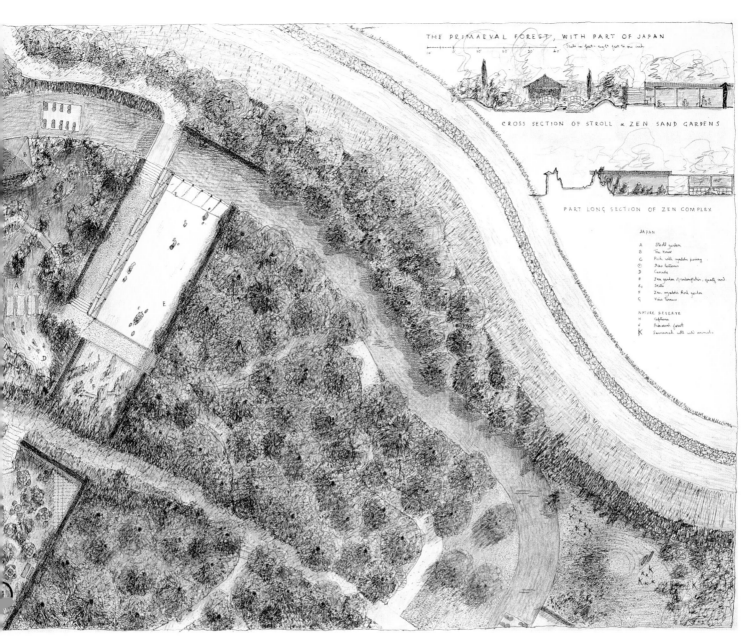

THE PRIMAEVAL FOREST, WITH PART OF JAPAN

CROSS SECTION OF STROLL & ZEN SAND GARDENS

PART LONG SECTION OF ZEN COMPLEX

JAPAN

A Stroll garden
B Tea house
C Park with myrtle fencing
Ⓒ Star lanterns
D Cascade
E Zen garden of contemplation, gravity sand
E₁ Seats
F Zen myoteki Rock garden
G View Terrace

NATURE RESERVE
H Cafeteria
J Primaeval forest
K Savannah with wild animals

Part of Japan; the Primaeval Forest

the stems of trees to borrow the waters of our own canal. We continue. Note the beach of specially chosen pebbles. The Stroll Garden, a microcosm of a Japanese earthly paradise, is derived from the Katsura Imperial Palace, 1620. First we see the pavilion in which the tea ceremony takes place. Then comes a glimpse of this wondrous garden of countless details: far away water emerges as a sparkling cascade from the mountains of the great divide; threads its way through the giant stepping stones of tourist man; and breaks into a tiny landscape of islands, bridges, stepping stones, stone lanterns and tables; symbolic paved paths; and lovely plants and little trees and moss. Then, too, a glimpse of the Zen-Buddhist Garden of Contemplation, Ryoan-Ji, 1488, the greatest endeavour made by mortal man to bring infinity to this earth. And so back through the primaeval forest and through the looking glass to where we began.

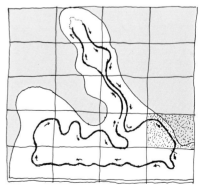

The return of the water-bus. Part of Japan; the Primaeval Forest

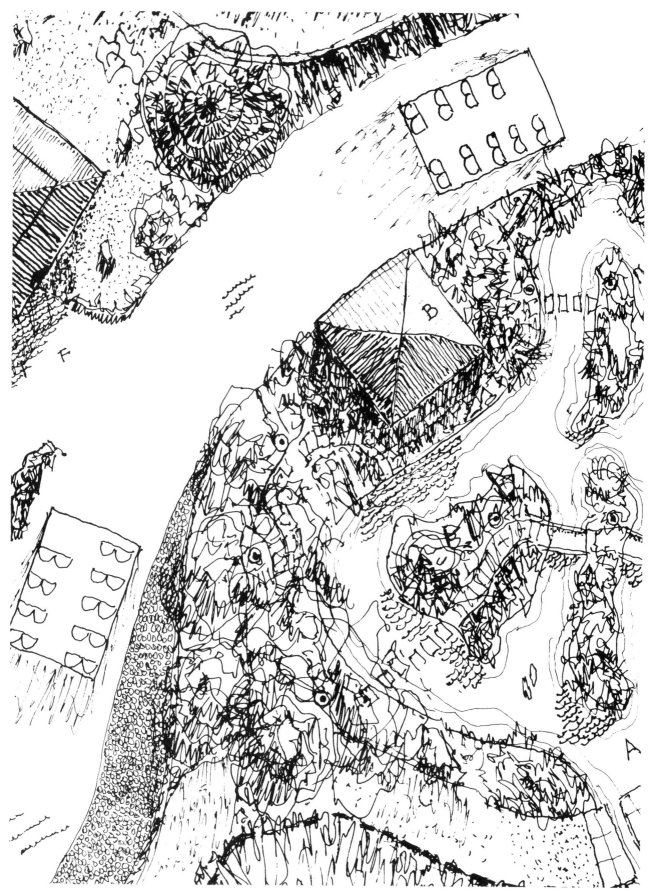

Japan — the Stroll Garden with the tea pavilion

Japan — the spirit of the Zen-Buddhist garden, Ryoan-Ji

Back to the beginning through the Primaeval Forest

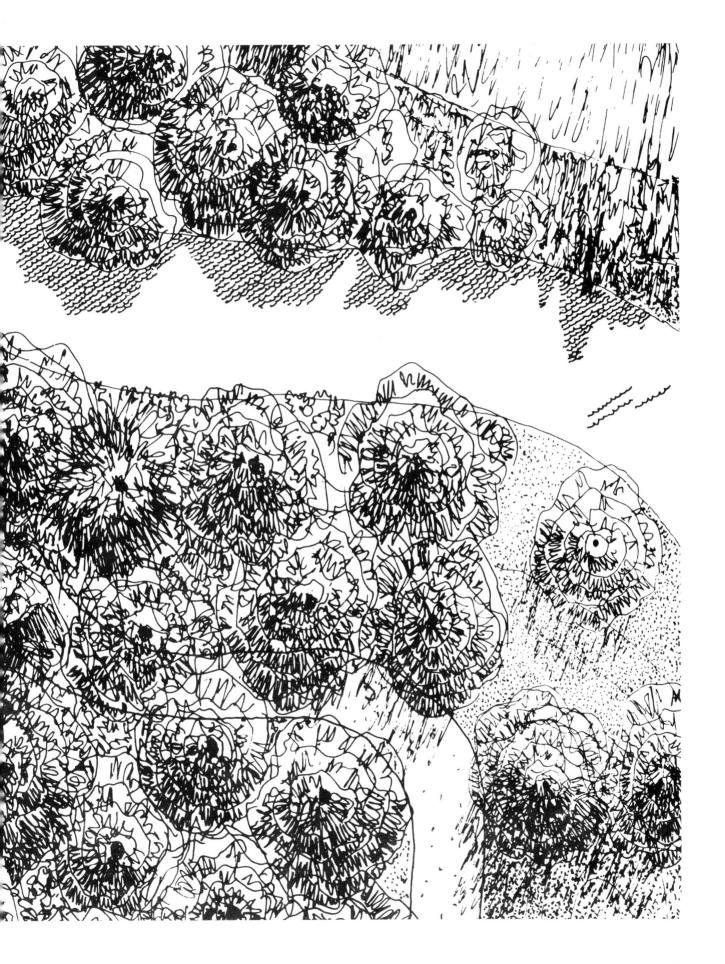

117

APPENDIX I
HOLLAND

In the selection of twelve basic cultures and four primaevals, a choice lay between nineteenth century England and seventeenth century Holland; a Dutch canal garden would follow the Italian Renaissance and the classical sequence would end, more truthfully to history, with seventeenth century France. On weighing the relative values the designer felt that the only indeterminate culture of the series, the English nineteenth century, had this important requisite: it linked history to the present age. This does not mean that the philosophic influence of Holland on history is of no account. On the contrary, if the modern public park can be traced back to the eighteenth century English aristocratic park (pages 44-45 and 52-63), so the conception of a garden for all as a political philosophy can be traced back to seventeenth century Holland. Although by its very nature no single Dutch garden can rank with the world's greatest, it seems agreeably symbolic that the prototype of the sequence of classical gardens should in fact be the Dutch canal linked with enchantingly geometric high-walled flower gardens. The rise of the Dutch republic meant a rise of the personal garden as dominant in all future landscape art. The reason is clear.

Holland in the seventeenth century was the birthplace of liberalism. Now free of Spanish domination materially and spiritually, it created within itself the first truly democratic society with complete freedom of personal speculation. When Descartes, who lived here for twenty years, declared, 'I think, therefore I am' he opened a vista of the human mind that has no end.

The modern personal garden responds to a vastly wider range of ideas than those of puritanical seventeenth century Holland, but perhaps for this very reason its roots are not so deep. Nevertheless, this saga of garden history can rightly be closed with a quote from the introduction to *The Landscape of Man:*

> All design derives from impressions of the past, conscious or unconscious, and in the modern collective landscape, from historic gardens and parks and silhouettes that were created for totally different social reasons derived from impressions of the world: the classical from the geometry of agriculture, the romantic from the natural landscape. *Only the small private garden remains true to its instinctive unchanged purpose of expressing, protecting and consoling the individual.*

The Avenue, Middelharnais, by Meyndert Hobbema, 1639-1709 (National Gallery, London)

'The painters of Holland were to have a profound effect on the way Western man saw the world about him. Political freedom allowed scientists and philosophers to develop new ideas, including the realisation that man was not the centre of the universe, but a fragment in the totality of nature. Even the most commonplace object now acquired a status. The men and women of Holland lived in neat brick houses and gardens. . . but the artists made them look beyond the planned environment'.

'The full significance and inherent beauty of the planet's atmosphere was unconsciously recognised by the Dutch painters of the seventeenth century, far in advance of science'.

(*The Landscape of Man*)

APPENDIX II

JUNG AND THE
MAGIC MOUNTAIN

'All the most powerful ideas in history go back to archetypes. This is particularly true of religious ideas, but the central concepts of science, philosophy and ethics are no exception to this rule. In their present form they are variants of archetypal ideas, created by consciously applying and adapting these ideas to reality. For it is the function of consciousness not only to recognise and assimilate the external world through the gateway of the senses, but to translate into visible reality the world within us.'
(Collected Works of Jung).

'Jung's belief in the ultimate unity of all existence led him to suppose that physical and mental, as well as spatial and temporal, were human categories imposed upon reality which did not accurately reflect it.'
(*Jung, Selected Writings,* Anthony Storr)

The Moody Historical Gardens are intended to be both 'a translation into visible reality of the world within us' and 'an expression of the ultimate unity of all existence'. Although not specifically mentioned by Jung, it is argued here that landscape cultures can also be traced to a single archetype or essence. In the Moody Gardens the source is the water (in China the *Yen*) and the corollary is the magic mountain (the *Yhan*). Together they are an abstract idea which unifies the disparate objects of the visible world.

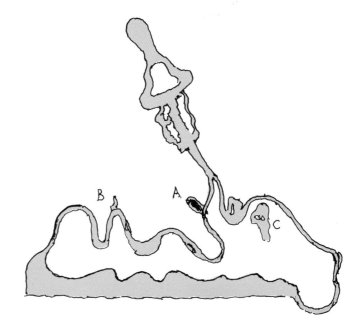

The abstract water pattern of the Moody Historical Gardens
A Mountain
B Waterfall
C Lake

⊢—⊣ 100 feet

The prototype of this project has been a garden of some three acres in south-west England, created over fifteen years from an historic setting and now sufficiently advanced to be effective. The water design is shown below. The source is a silent timeless pool at the highest point fed by a perpetual spring. The waters flow downward in two routes to feed seven garden 'visible realities'. The waters then merge and pass from woodlands to open landscape. Three descending pools respond to an ancient fish pond; over all is the sound of water. Although this English garden is an expression of individual taste and philosophy, and the Moody Gardens are collective, yet the principle of the unification of diverse subjects through the subconscious is the same.

Having now accepted the archetype-theory of water as 'the thread of truth', let us consider the many secondary instances where the subconscious has been used to reinforce the visible. Perhaps these are categories 'imposed upon reality which did not accurately reflect it'.

The principle is that a hidden meaning is given to a particular landscape when a heightened emotion is required. The meaning is expressed in shape and form; that is to say the emotions of delight, fear, horror, sex, religion or what you will, can be aroused by a subconscious association of ideas in either the present or the deep past. In order for this to be effective, it is essential that the conscious mind, the intellect, is unaware of what has passed into it through 'the gateway of the senses'. If revealed, the impact may be one of sentimentality. In practice such curious secrets cannot always be kept. Readers of this guide will already have been given clues as to the meaning of the rock facing Eden and the mountain range of the great divide. There are others that shrewd observers can detect from the drawings, if not in reality; and still others that even the designer himself cannot detect.

So important is it that landscape of this kind is designed for the two levels of the mind that, overleaf, is debated the relative values of a piece of rock made by nature and a work made by man that common sense tells us should replace it. But should it?

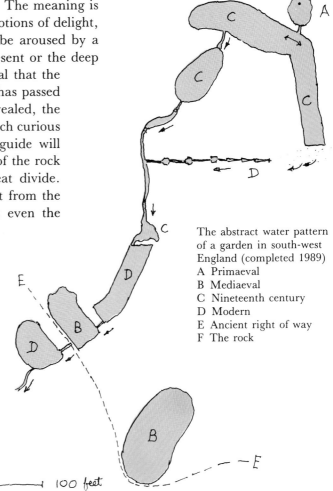

The abstract water pattern of a garden in south-west England (completed 1989)
A Primaeval
B Mediaeval
C Nineteenth century
D Modern
E Ancient right of way
F The rock

100 feet

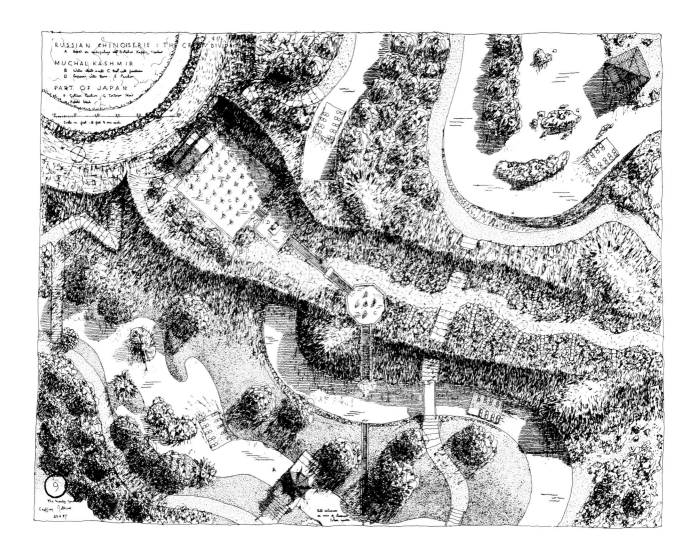

THE CASE FOR THE MUGHAL GARDEN

The Islamic gardens of India and Spain are represented in the Moody Gardens only by their source: the so-called Persian paradise garden. Is this not unfair, especially to the Mughal gardens of Kashmir, set in the heart of the Himalayas? The empty space within the mountain of the great divide is surely calling to be filled with a Mughal design that will establish its right to a place in history. The proposed design fits neatly into the mountains, is academically correct in the spirit of its geometry, and is ingeniously linked to the Islam garden in the classical sequence. Admittedly, the passengers in the water-bus will only see the rivulet and the water chute as they pass, but this will tempt them to visit on foot one of the most spectacular concepts of a garden that the world has known. *This is the case of humanist and historian.*

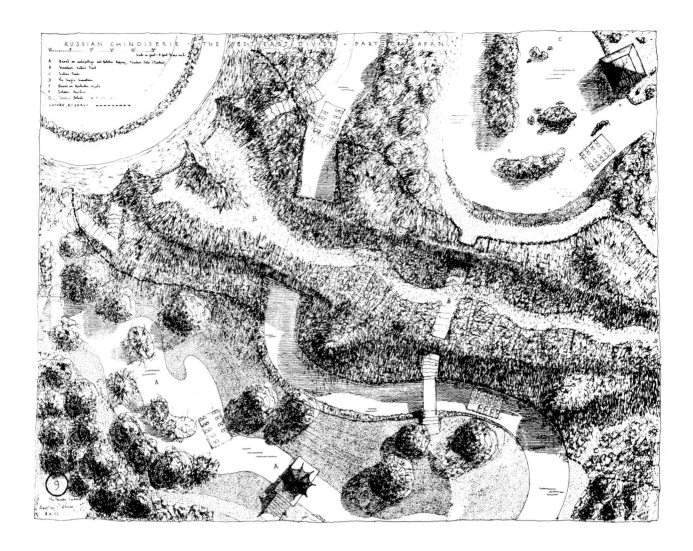

THE CASE FOR THE MAGIC MOUNTAIN

From Sinai to Meru and Fiji all mountains are magic to the human race. Our own is named after *The Magic Mountain* of Thomas Mann, who explored the two levels of the mind to convey 'the seeds of Time' to the reader. The purpose of our own mountain cannot be conveyed by any drawing, so let me guide you as in reality. As you approach from any one of five ways, you are unconsciously being conditioned to an environment very different from the humanised 'flat' lands below. You are at the beginning of creation. You see before you an unscalable rock and behind it the primaeval wet-lands, sea and sky. Your body may not be able to scale the rock, but your imagination can. On the summit you can, if you are so inclined, experience Lucretius' great didactic poem on creation, *De Rerum Natura* (On the Nature of Things) and see our planet as others see it. For all its scars it is a goodly planet. *This is the case of poet and philosopher, and of me, the designer.*

PART 2

FURTHER STUDIES
OF THE
WESTERN CLASSICAL SEQUENCE

The smallness of the areas allocated
to the western classical cultures is
justified only if the contents of each box,
like Shakespeare's Wooden O, can
suggest greater worlds beyond. The art
of each, highly stylised, is intensely
concentrated and for this reason calls for
a more precise study than that of the
generalised cultures.

During these deeper studies it was
inevitable that fresh ideas evolved and
that these should call for minor
variations. These are recorded.

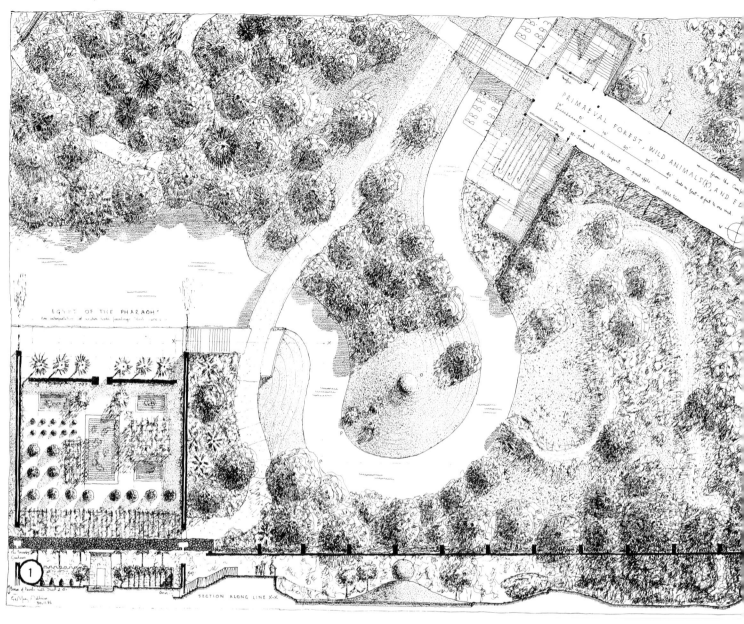

Eden — the original plan page 24

Water

The prospect of an illuminated procession of boats on summer evenings called for a storage water-park, and this has taken the place of the wildlife park, north of, and below, the approach from the campus.

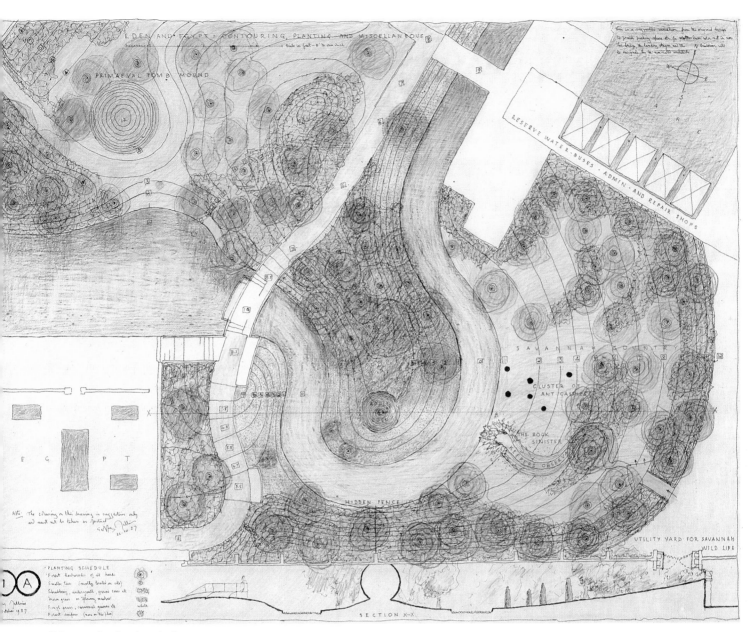

Eden — the developed plan

The Landscape of the Apple

The apple has been increased from 8 feet to 15 feet diameter. The wild landscape to the east has been remodelled to form an amphitheatre containing a shortened serpent, ant castles, and wild animals yet to be chosen, whose night quarters would be behind the perimeter wall facing the works yard.

View Balconies

Added to bridge and path.

Prehistoric Burial Mound

Added to the primaeval forest.

The approach to the island of Sark, the Channel Islands

Rock Sculpture

The whole shape of the lonely island of Sark is that of a prehistoric monster spread-eagled in the sea. The cliffs that tower above the port are particularly sinister and awe-inspiring.

It is vital that the rock opposite Eden should not be recognisable immediately as a serpent's head, but only of something sinister as an abstract shape. If recognisable the subject becomes sentimental and the objective purpose destroyed.

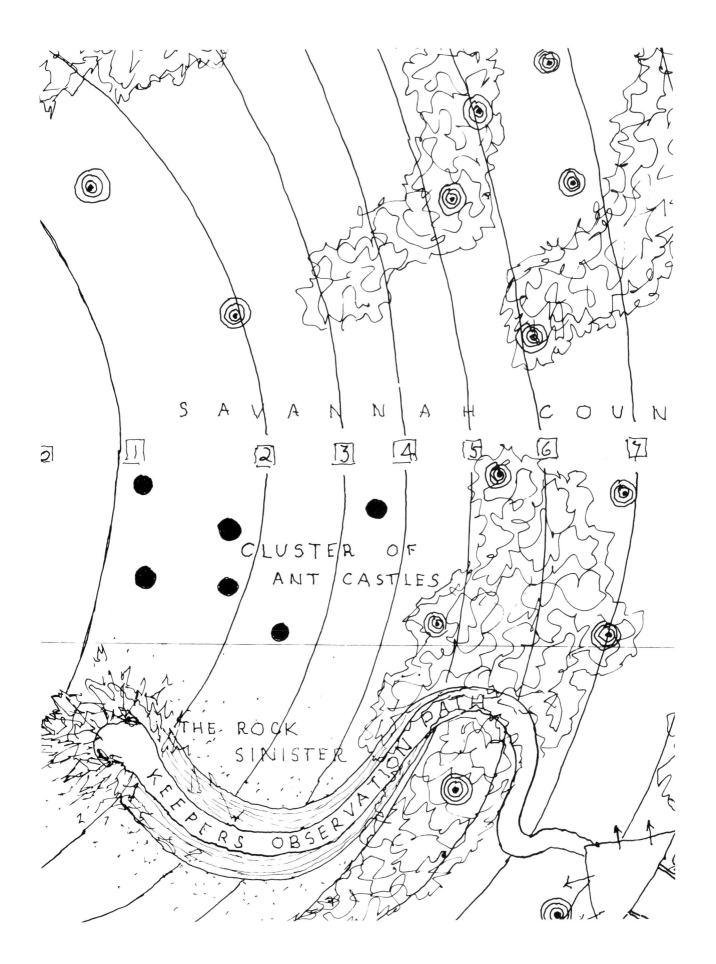

SAVANNAH COUN

CLUSTER OF
ANT CASTLES

THE ROCK
SINISTER

KEEPERS OBSERVATION PA

The concept of the Apple of Eden as imagined by the sculptor Angela Conner

The Moss Apple

In reality, the apple will have a diameter of 15 feet, and technically the moss surface will be left damp by an ingenious system of watering from the interior.

The increase in size from the original design came about when it was realised that, with Greece and China, it would form one point in a triangle of religions now at peace one with another.

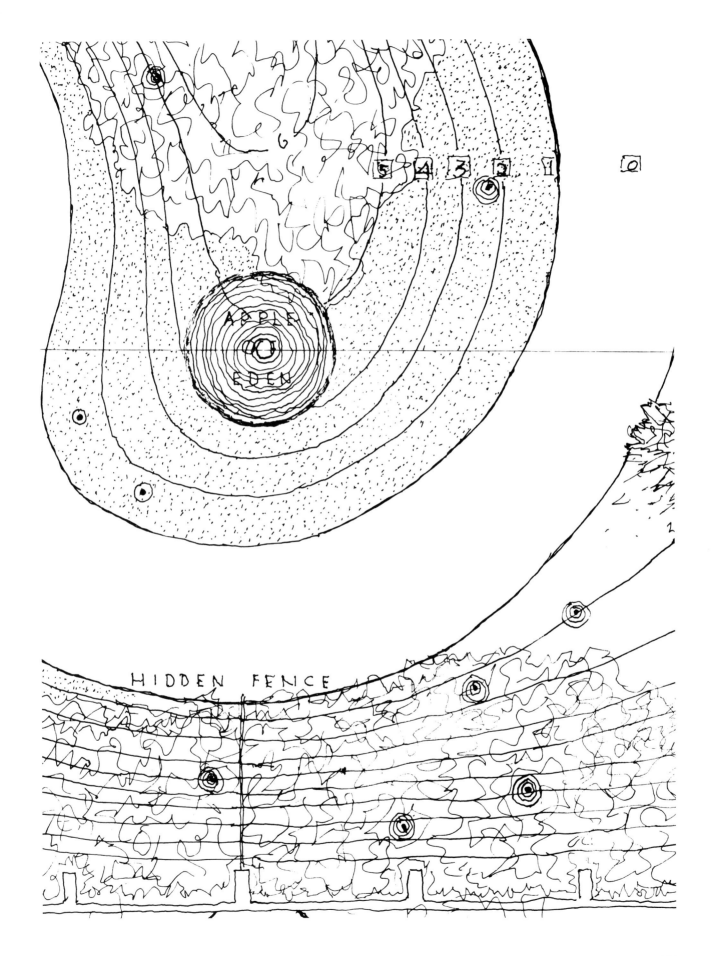

The Three Barrows by the painter John Piper

Burial Mound

It is appropriate that a burial mound be added to the primaeval landscape since it was the first monumental expression of man endeavouring to identify himself and his future in a hostile world. The desire to immortalise himself in this way seems to have been universal, and reached its climax in the Pyramid, a stupendous abstract of the mound illustrated above.

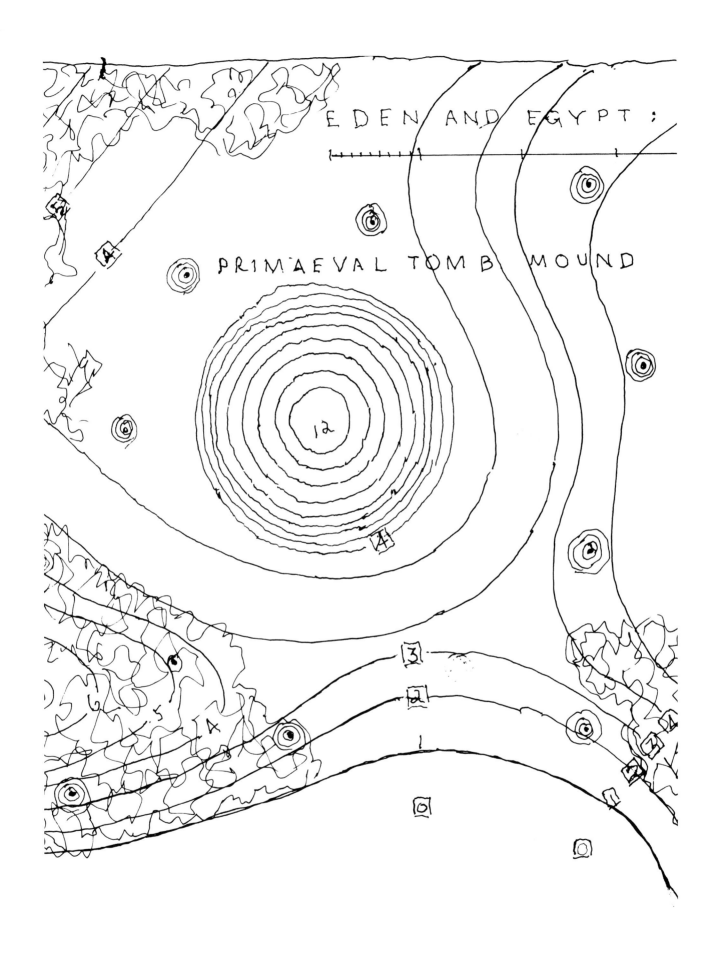

EDEN AND EGYPT:

PRIMAEVAL TOMB MOUND

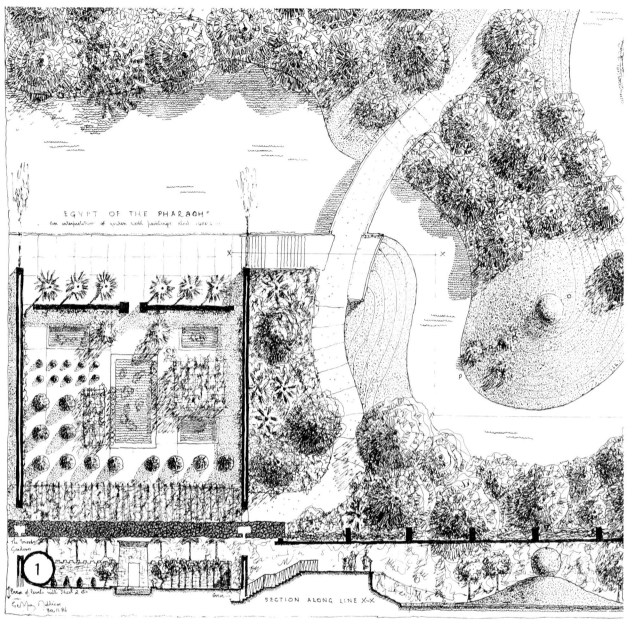

Egypt and the Bridge, the original plan page 24

Egypt

The proportions have been adjusted, but otherwise there is no change. It is interesting that in detailing this design there was no opportunity for development in depth. Like architecture, the structure of garden design had reached a finality and thereafter remained static for centuries. This freezing of the arts is unique in history, for the other apparently static major civilisation, China, was always in the imperceptible movement of the Tao, or 'the Way'.

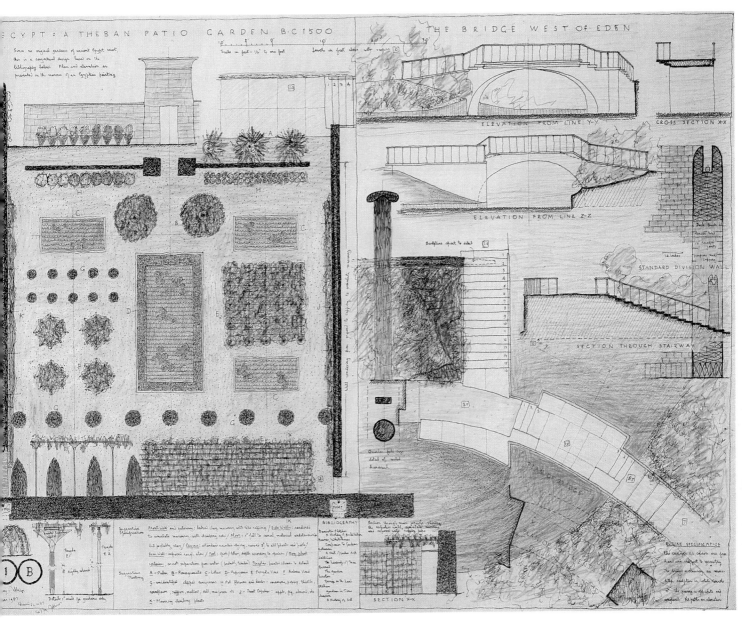

Egypt and the Bridge as detailed

The Bridge

Outside Egypt the details tell a different story, that of the turmoil of the adjoining Mesopotamia, where everything was in flux (as it is today). The bridge stands as a fulcrum between this scene and the ordered classical sequence that lies ahead. It is a white monolithic structure, roughly textured, with no identifiable historic style, and has been developed to comprehend a viewing balcony of the future in addition to that of the past. Also shown is the classical dividing wall (see page 190) and a section of the bronze handrail.

Conjectural restoration of a Theban garden by Charles Chipiez, 1883

ancient Egypt exist,
sed on the
elevation are
Egyptian painting

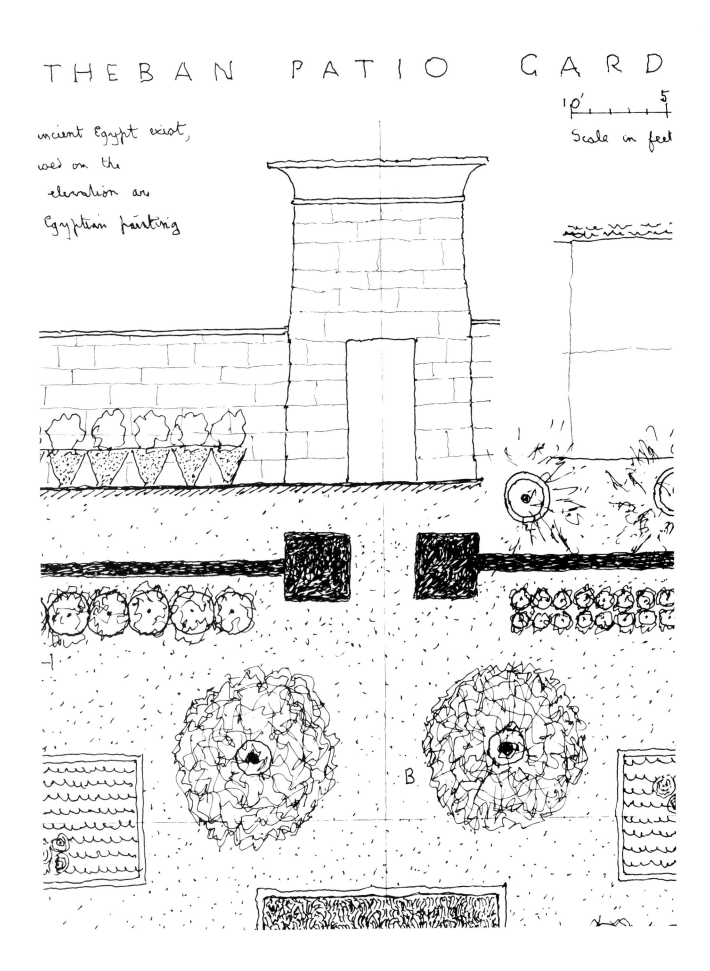

B

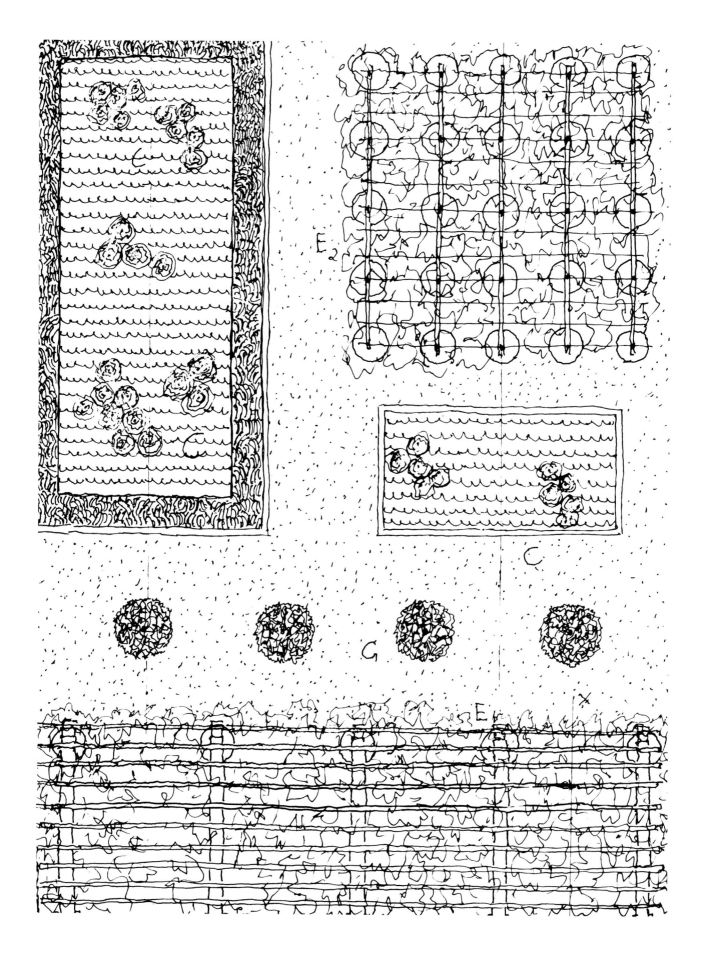

Garden scene from a tomb at Thebes

The garden is surrounded by a wall, probably tile-capped, and divided into unequal portions by low walls, about two feet high, of dry stone or baked mud, with painted wooden gates. The entrance from the tree-shaded canal-walk passes a grandiose porter's lodge; the house is reached by a path under the central vine trellis. On both sides of the house are pavilions overlooking flowers and pools planted with lotus and teeming with wild ducks. Inside the surrounding wall is a screen of date-palms, down-palms and smaller trees. (From *The Landscape of Man*)

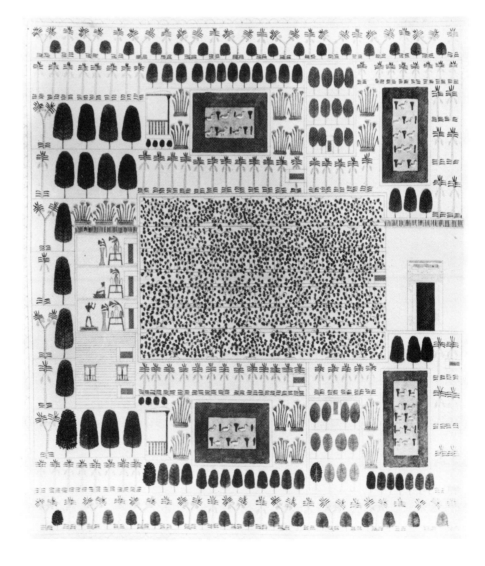

Plan of a garden estate of a wealthy Egyptian official

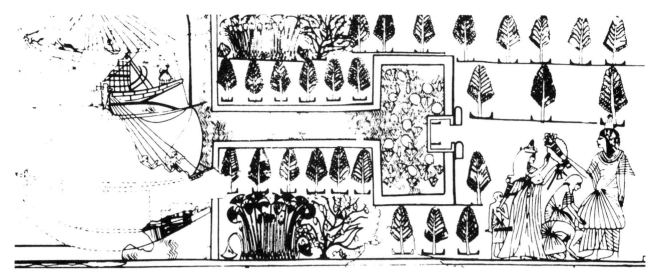

Tomb paintings. Above from the tomb of King Neperhotep. Below c BC1415

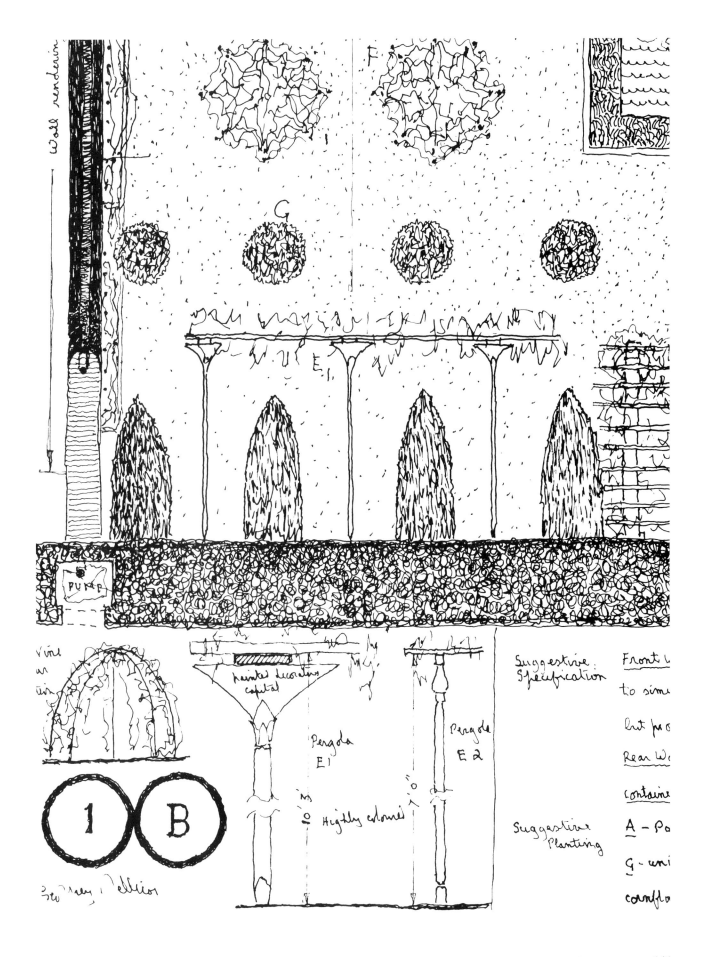

Wall rendering

F

G

E,

PUMP

Suggestive
Specification

Front w
to sime
but pro
Rear W
containe
A – Po
G – uni
cornflo

Vine
in
rin

painted decorative
capital

Pergola
E1

Pergola
E2

Highly coloured

1 B

Suggestive
Planting

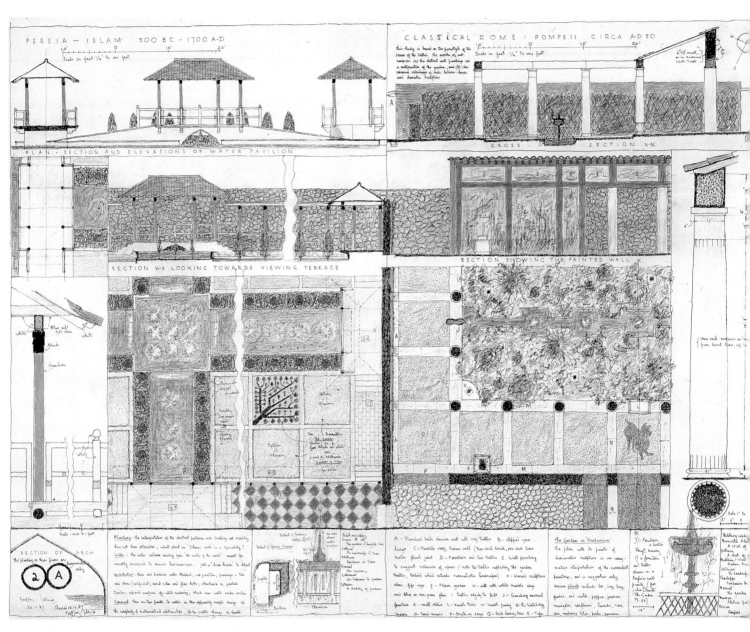

Classical Rome followed by Islam as detailed

The House of the Vettii, Pompeii

The wall paintings have been reduced in number, and the rear of the wall facing the long corridor emulates Hadrian's great brick wall at Tivoli. See pages 144 and 145 for the dog mosaic.

The Paradise Garden

Unchanged, but attention is drawn to the play of ripples on the water surface, caused by bubble rather than high jet fountains. The translation of abstract tree patterns into reality has yet to be resolved.

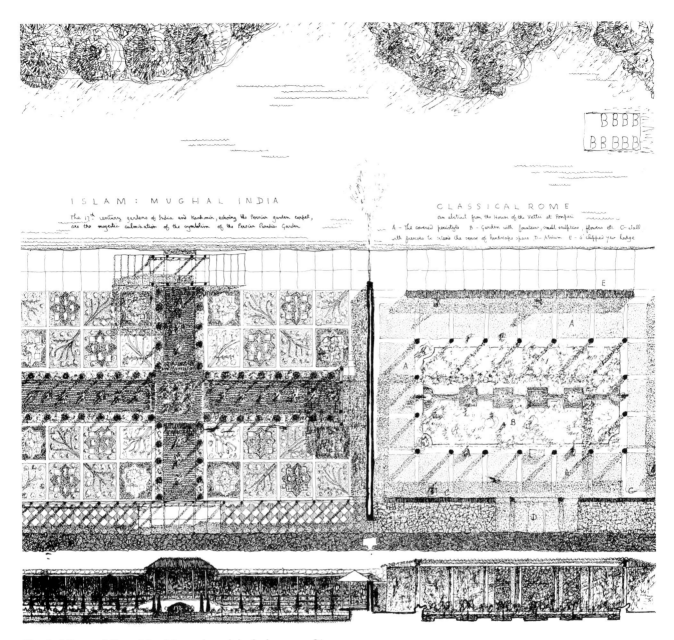

ISLAM : MUGHAL INDIA

The 17th century gardens of India and Kashmir, echoing the Persian garden carpet, are the majestic culmination of the symbolism of the Persian Paradise Garden

CLASSICAL ROME

an abstract from the House of the Vettii at Pompeii

A – The covered peristyle   B – Garden with fountains, small sculptures, flowers etc   C – Wall with frescoes to create the sense of landscape space   D – Atrium   E – 6' clipped yew hedge

Classical Rome followed by Islam, the original plan page 31

   The two gardens are roughly parallel in time (early AD), but totally dissimilar in character. While the Paradise garden scarcely changed its symbolic form throughout the ages, the Roman garden of Pompeii was purely secular, intensely virile intellectually, and very much in the fashion of the moment.

The Peristyle Garden in the House of the Vettii, Pompeii, before AD79

Pompeii
Since these designs were made more details have been revealed about the garden plans; the present design is conjectural.

The mosaic on the floor, showing the dog guarding the entrance, is traditional

Cave canem (beware of the dog), Pompeii

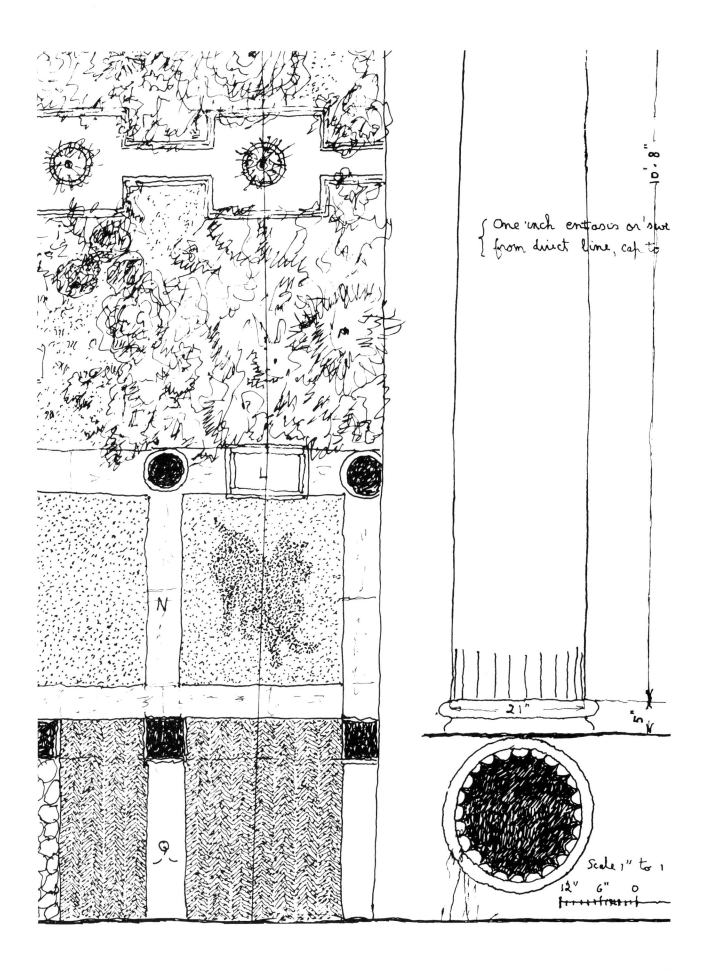

One 'inch entasis or 'swe
from direct line, cap to

8' 0"

5"

21"

L

N

Scale 1" to 1

12" 6" 0

Cross-view of the Peristyle Garden, the House of the Vettii, Pompeii

Pompeian wall painting

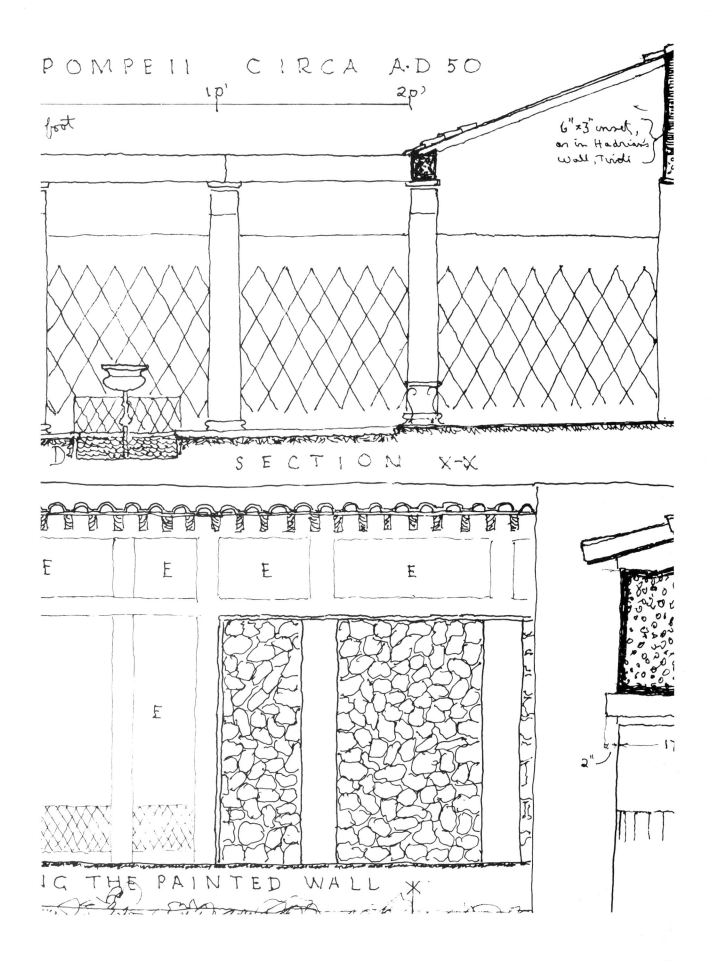

POMPEII   CIRCA A·D·50

10'   20'

foot

6"x3" onset,
as in Hadrian's
Wall, Tivoli

D

S E C T I O N   X–X

E   E   E   E

E

2"   17

...G   THE   PAINTED   WALL

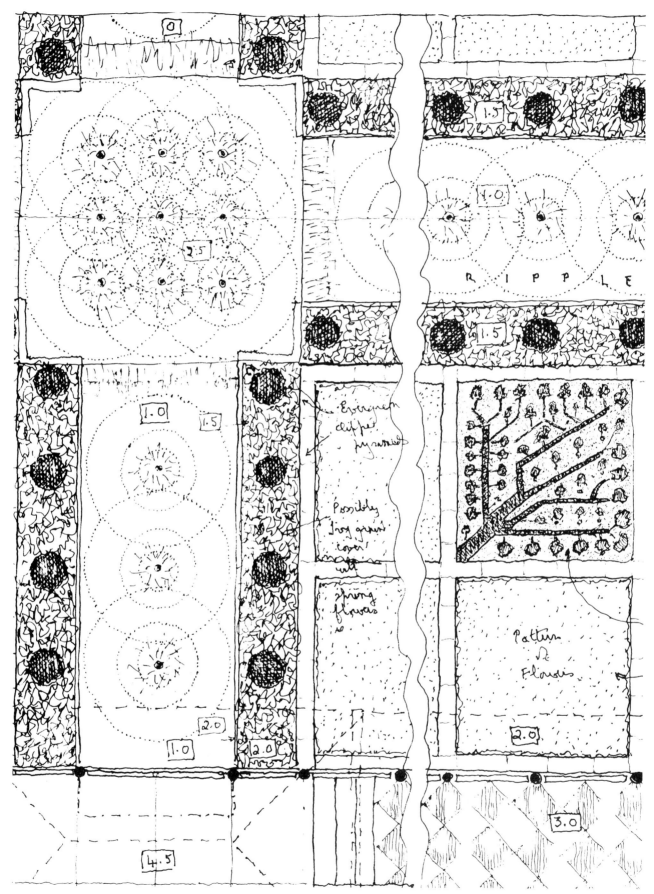

Detail of canal, fountains and planting pattern

The origin of the seventeenth century carpet can be traced to the Spring Carpet of Chosroes, one of the glories of Ctesiphon, about AD 300. This is a similar carpet

The Paradise pattern is common to all Islamic gardens, but the architecture changes with each century. The illustrations are of Achabal, Kashmir, seventeenth century

1,0'   0   10'   20'

Scale in feet ¼" to one foot

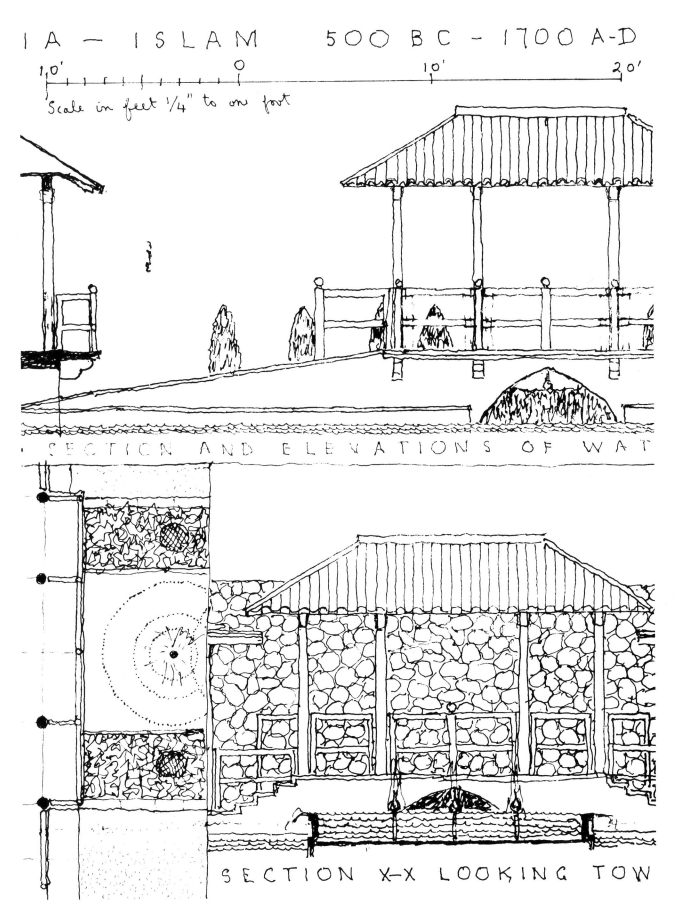

SECTION AND ELEVATIONS OF WAT

SECTION X-X LOOKING TOW

Top, viewing walkway; above, part of sea wall

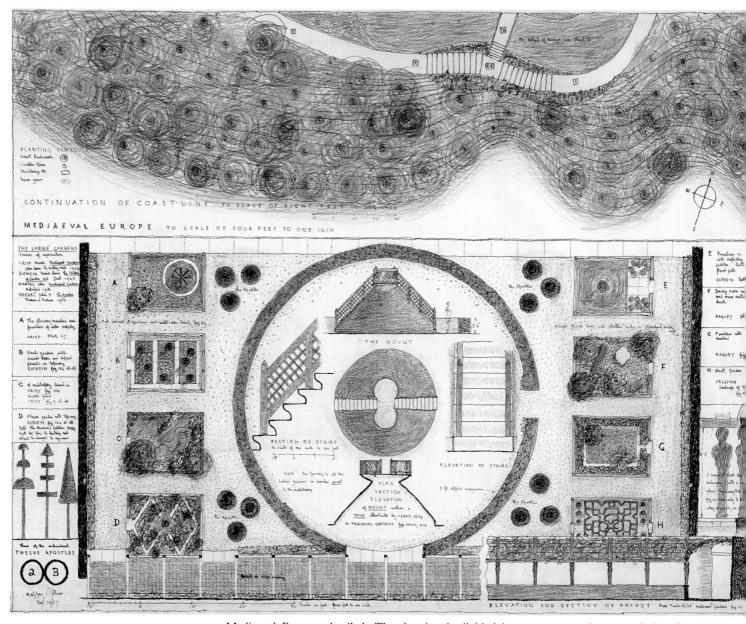

Mediaeval Europe, detailed. The drawing is divided into two parts, the upper being the contouring and tree planting of the north bank and is to half scale

The only significant variation is that the whole design has been translated into the concept of the Sermon on the Mount. The ominous clipped yew at each corner of the maze has been displaced by three apostles, clipped trees beloved of the Middle Ages and as different one from another as is chalk from cheese. On the mount the pulpit.

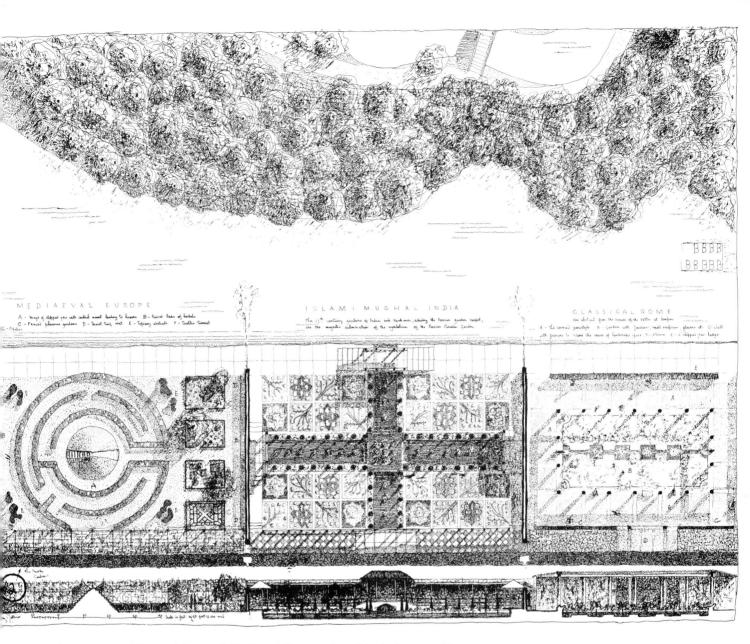

The sequence of Rome, Islam and Mediaeval Europe, the original plan page 31

While there is little sympathy between Rome and the Paradise Garden of the Middle East, there is distinct affinity between the latter and mediaeval Europe. In different ways both landscapes shown above are metaphysical. The four rivers geometry of the one symbolises heaven brought to earth, whereas the circle and the mound indicate man groping upwards to heaven — not unlike the Mesopotamian Ziggurat at the summit of which man could converse with the gods.

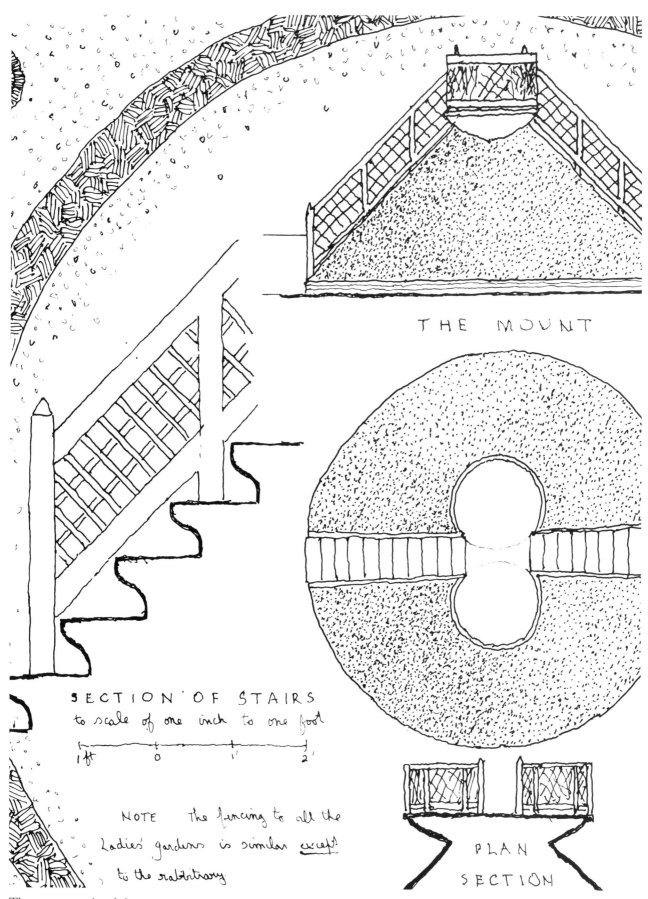

THE MOUNT

SECTION OF STAIRS
to scale of one inch to one foot

1 ft 0 1' 2

NOTE   The fencing to all the
Ladies' gardens is similar except
to the rabbitrary

PLAN
SECTION

The mount and pulpit

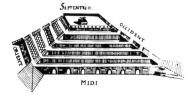

Maze from *Mediaeval Gardens* by Frank Crisp

Examples of maze designs

Gardens at Wadham College, Oxford, showing the conical mount

Sacred maze from *Mediaeval Gardens* by Frank Crisp

155

One of the two famous paintings (c1410-20) by a master from the Upper Rhine. This provides the best evidence for mediaeval plantsmanship. The use, in combination, of trees, border flowers, and smaller plants, displays a tradition quite distinct from that of small beds set between paths or grass lawns

Convent garden, with two small gardens enclosed with delicate lattice-work. 'The Holy Family', Joseph is omitted, on left. Early sixteenth century. Note the treatment of garden and wall; sometimes the flower border is replaced by raised turf seats

The Ladies' Gardens (opposite). In a hostile country the tiny miniatures of an idyllic world outside were precious to the ladies hemmed securely within the castle walls. Nowhere in the western world is there such tenderness between the individual plant and the individual woman (not the man)

E The mediaeval instructions for the fountain were: 'As clear as crystal, its waters flowing over silver pebbles, ever fresh and glistening... a magic mirror, so that you can see half the garden in it, and if you look up, there is the same picture to be seen again.' (*History of Garden Art,* M L Gothein)

F An interpretation of the top picture

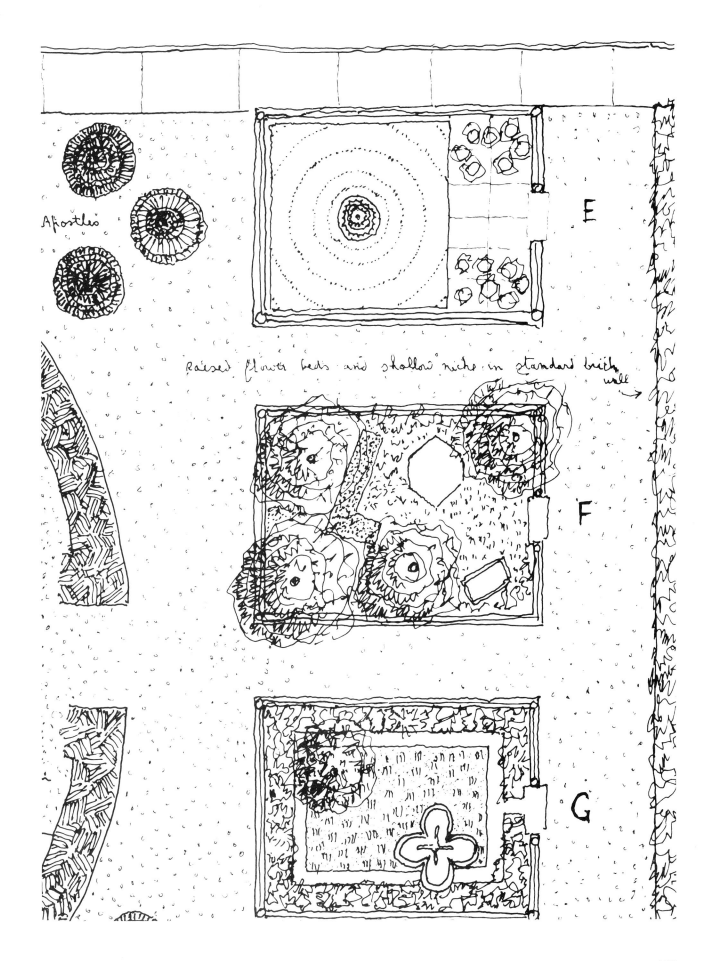

Apostles

E

Raised flower beds and shallow niches in standard brick wall

F

G

Above, herb garden with raised
beds and clipped plants. Right,
rabbitary surrounded by a
wattle fence. These features are
included in the detail opposite

158

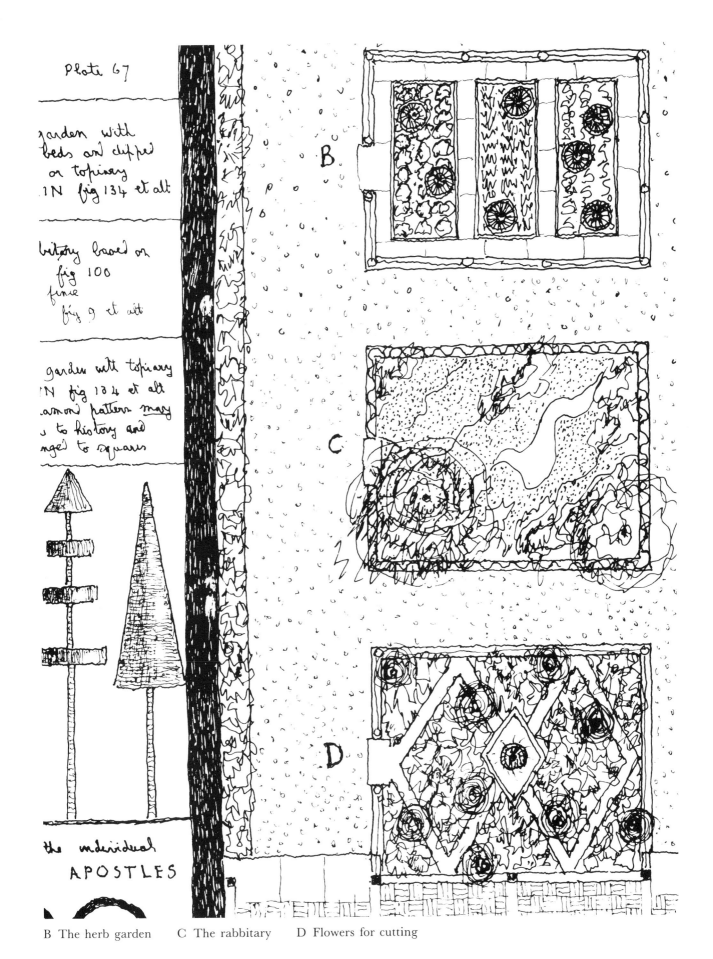

Plate 67

garden with
beds and clipped
or topiary
IN fig 134 et alt

bitany based on
fig 100
fence
fig 9 et alt

garden with topiary
IN fig 134 et alt
amon' pattern may
v to history and
nge' to squares

B

C

D

the individual
APOSTLES

B The herb garden   C The rabbitary   D Flowers for cutting

Above, mediaeval tree
decoration. Above
right, a Mary garden.
Right, summer garden
of Crispin de Pass
1614. The detail of the
long arcade opposite is
based on this print.

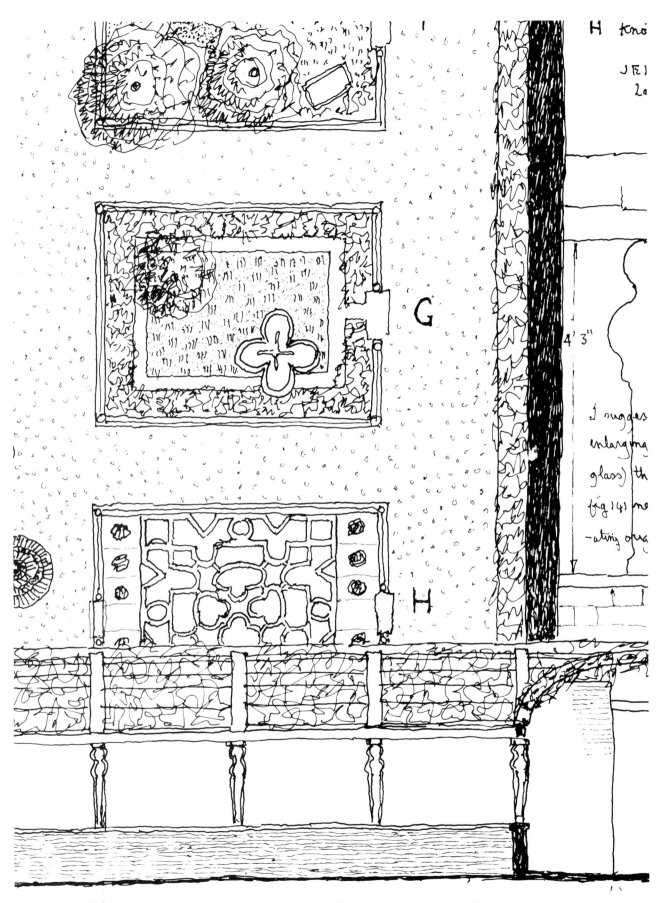

The following handwritten annotations appear on the drawing:

H kno

JE1
2a

4' 3"

I sugges
enlarging
glass) th
fig 14) ne
-ating ova

The Ladies' Gardens. G Interpretation of the print opposite. H A knot garden of box.
The arcade taken from the print opposite

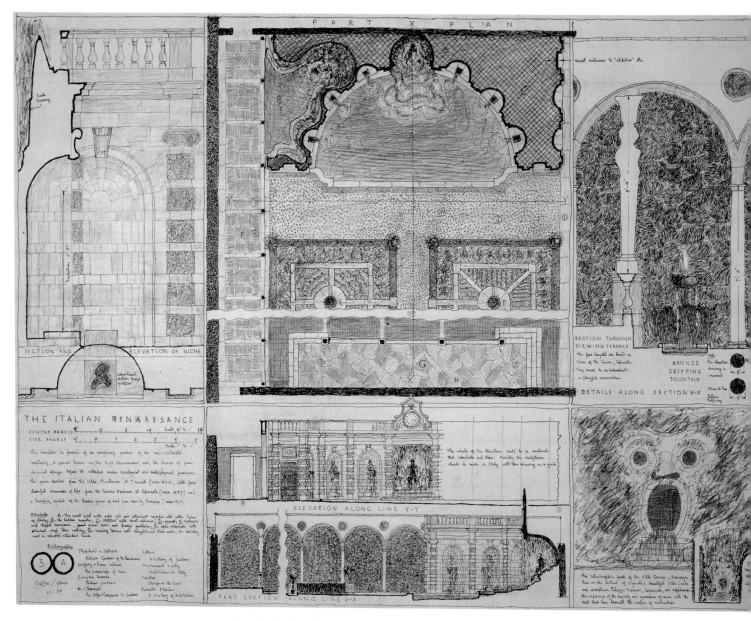

The Italian Renaissance; details

There is an addition to the original that is alarming to adults but highly pleasurable to children. This is the monster imported from Bomarzo (page 171) to fill the secret void behind the great semi-circle. His purpose is to disrupt the placid architecture of the time, and, by inference, the civilisation.

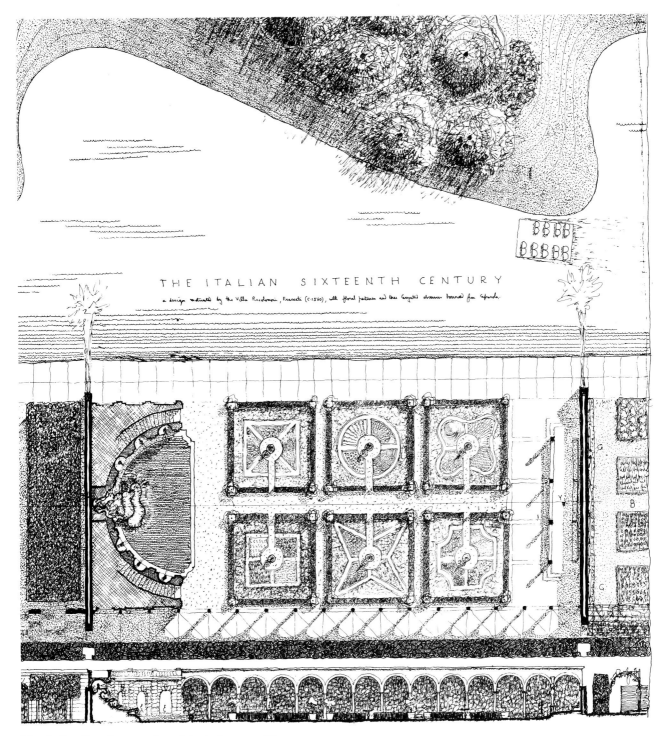

THE ITALIAN SIXTEENTH CENTURY

a design motivated by the Villa Picadomini, Frascati (c.1560), with floral parterres and trees (angeli) strewn toward for Sferada.

The Italian Renaissance, the original plan page 38

Although the squares of the parterre indicate a decisive geometry, the proportions elsewhere are arbitrary. The endeavour has been to enter the mind of an architect of the time, who would undoubtedly have designed by 'feeling' and left to posterity the extraction of the mathematics of the proportions, if any.

163

The Villa Piccolomini at
Frascati, as measured by
Shepherd and Jellicoe in 1924.
The Great Water Pavilion has
been interpreted to a scale
reduced to a relative proportion
of 5:3

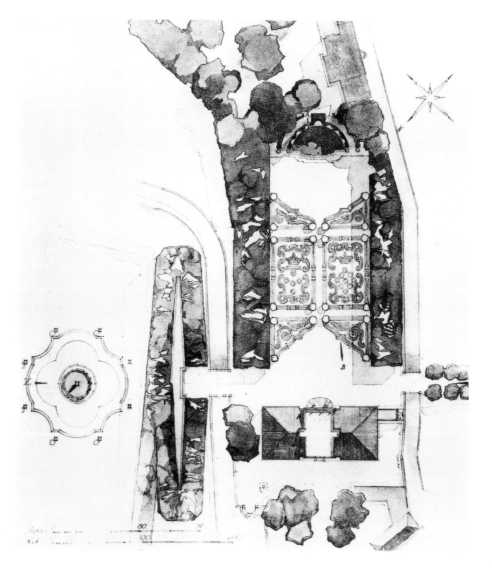

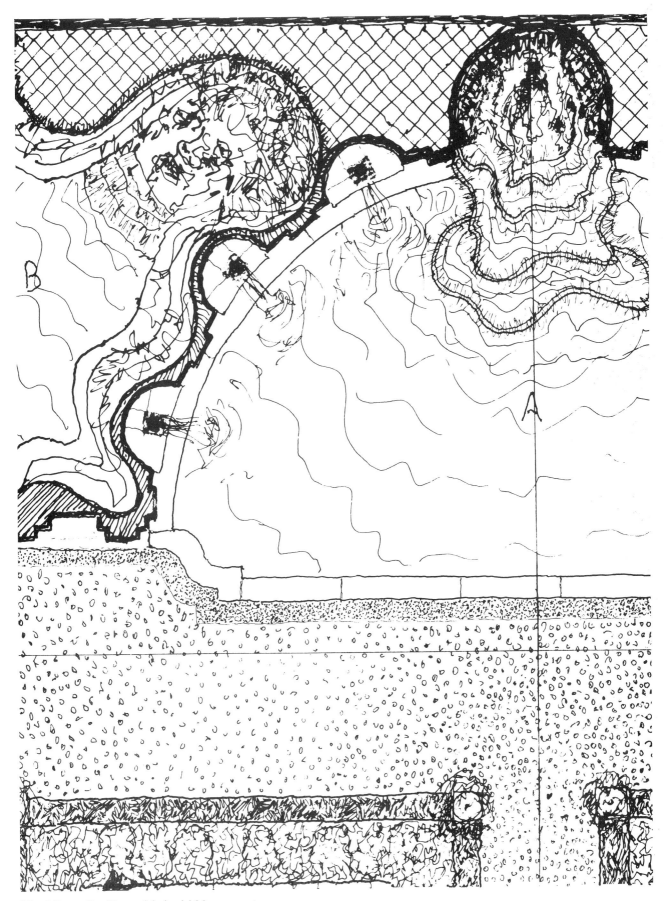

The Water Pavilion with its hidden monster

The Villa Piccolomini at Frascati, 1924, severely damaged in World War II

The pavilion, Villa Piccolomini, Frascati

SECTION AND   ELEVATION OF NICHE

noch
Scenery

Sculpture 6' 8"

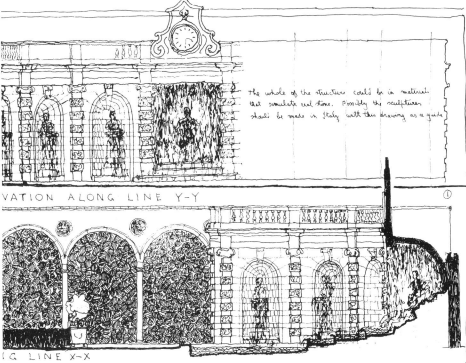

The whole of the structure could be in materials
that simulate real stone. Possibly the sculptures
should be made in Italy with this drawing as a guide

VATION ALONG LINE Y-Y   ①

G LINE X-X

Detail of the corner of the
pavilion, enlarged from a
photograph of 1924. The detail
has been modified to
accommodate the change of
scale

8'-4"

7'-9"

SECTION THROUGH
VIEWING TERRACE

Details of the Casino garden of the Farnese Palace, Caprarola, from photographs taken by
Shepherd and Jellicoe in 1924

A giant from the Villa Orsini, Bomarzo

The near-contemporary grotto of the Boboli Gardens, Florence, by Buontalenti, suggestive of surrealism

The monster from the Villa Orsini, Bomarzo, known as 'the Gate of Hell' and perhaps the most frightening of all the monsters that challenged the supremacy of man. The contemporary gardens of the lovely Villa Lante by Vignola, are in the neighbourhood

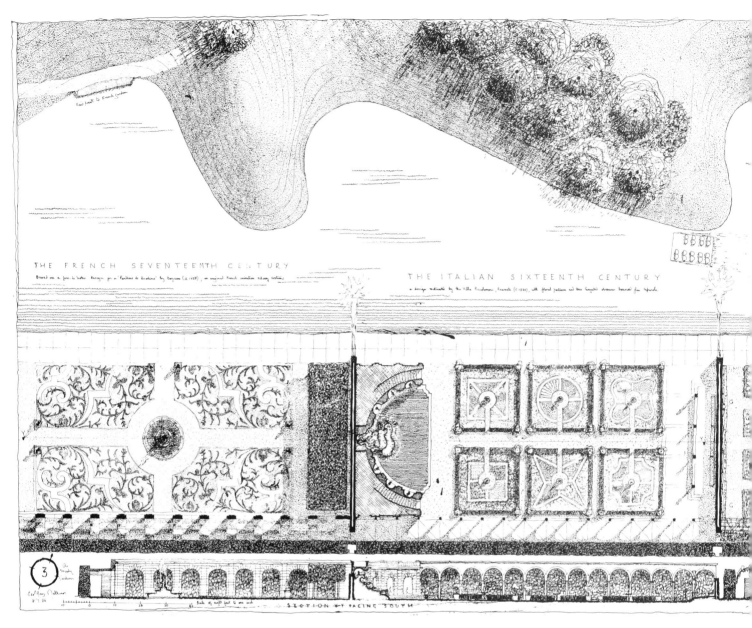

THE FRENCH SEVENTEENTH CENTURY

Based on a pen-&-water design for a "Parterre de Broderie" by Boyceau (d. 1638), an original French invention arising circa 1600

THE ITALIAN SIXTEENTH CENTURY

a design indicated by the Villa Piccolomini, Frascati (c. 1560), with formal parterres and trees (cypressi) drawn-in boxed-in from Capriola

③ ...

SECTION Y-Y FACING SOUTH

The French Seventeenth Century; the original plan page 38

The concept of classical landscape reached a climax under Le Nôtre, at no time in its history has there been so great an elegance, beauty, planning technique and superficiality. Not for the Sun King the constant reminder, as in Italy, of the monster growling below — the monster that was later to surface and swallow the monarchy whole.

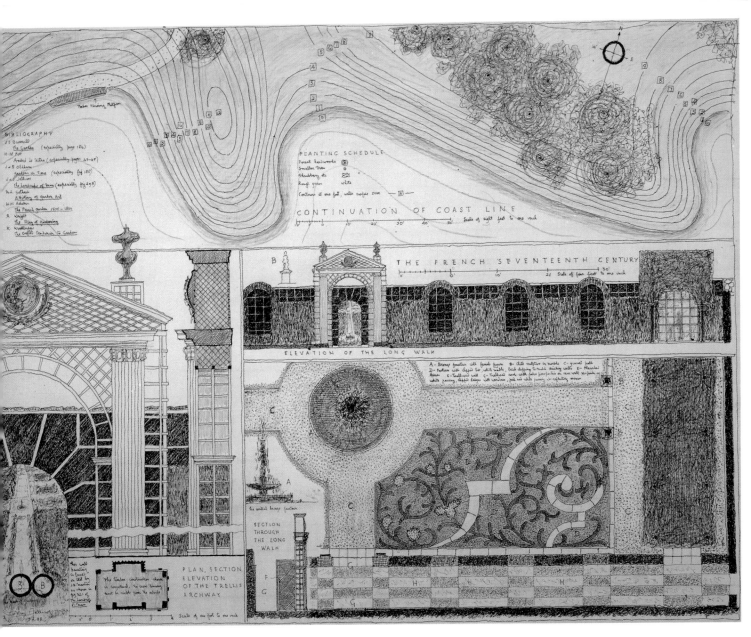

The French Seventeenth Century; the details

There has been a major change in the long arcade, which did not seem to do justice to the essential elegance and inventiveness of the period. There is a central trellis portico, clipped windowed evergreen walls, black marbled rear wall, and a reflecting mirror at the end of each clipped lime walk. The portico leads to a false perspective of Versailles.

Top, trellis work designed by
Perelle.
Middle, sketch for a palisade at
the Trianon.
Below, sketch for the palisade
of the Thèâtre de l'Eau at
Versailles

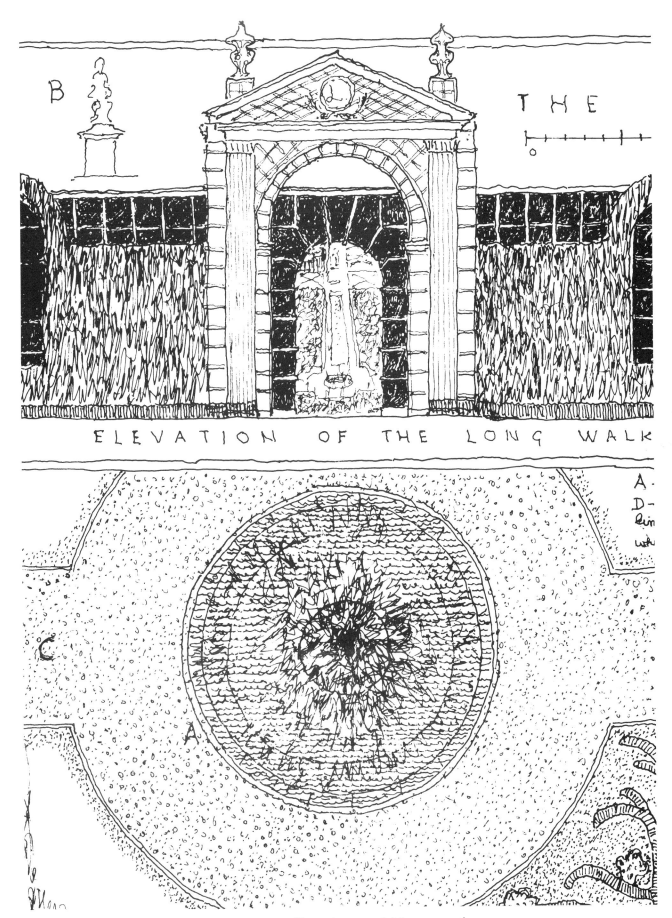

ELEVATION OF THE LONG WALK

Plan of the central fountain, and (above) the trellis archway and false perspective
of Versailles

Top, Compartiment de Broderie by Boyceau (d1638) executed in box, coloured sands and flowers. This is the chosen design but without the flowers. Bottom, the main parterre of Vaux-le-Vicomte, with clipped box and red brick-dust (from *Gardens in Time,* Oldham)

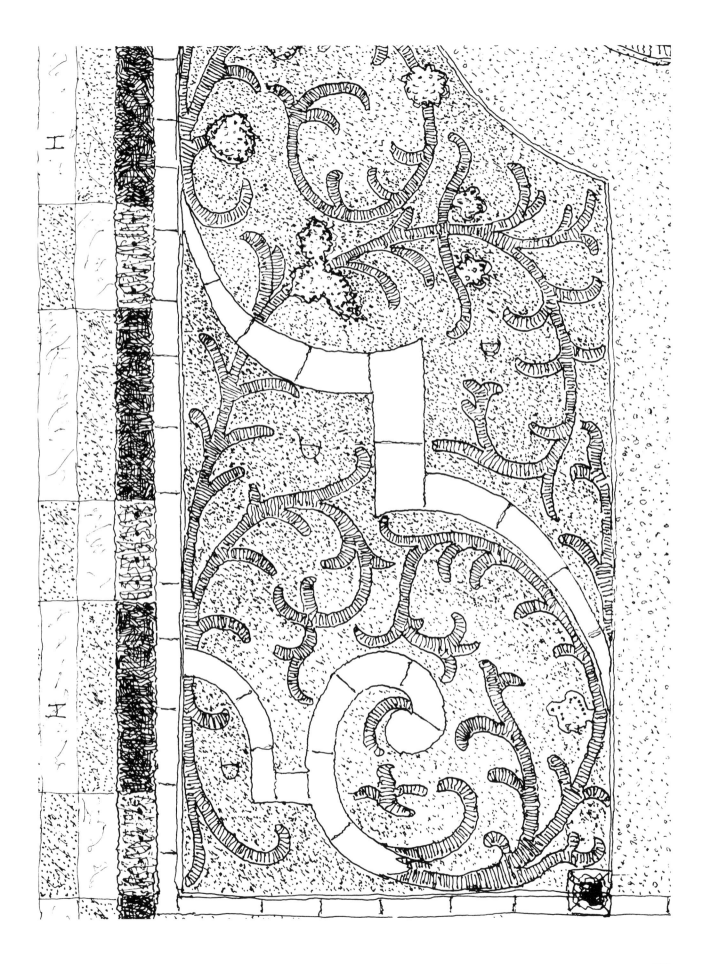

The early eighteenth century gardens of Champs as reconstructed by Henri Duchesne. The parterre framed by clipped limes, beneath which one walks in the heat of the day, is essentially in the French tradition

The black marble wall behind the green windows, and the reflecting mirror at the end of the pleached walk

SEVENTEENTH CENTURY

0'   20   Scale of four feet to one inch   30'

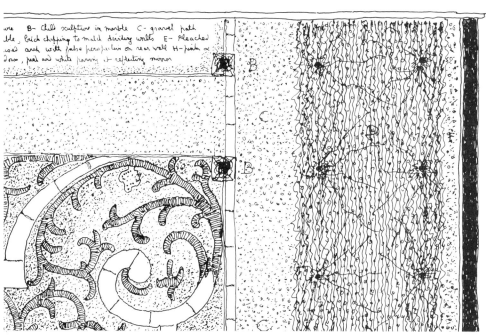

Detail of the trellis archway

Eighteenth century trellis in the gardens of Schönbrunn, Vienna, as existing in 1931. There are few, if any, French seventeenth century examples existing, for the material is fragile. In interpreting trellis into reality, the visual penetration of form is unique to architecture, and must not be spoiled by such internal structure that may be necessary for stability

The English Nineteenth Century, the details. The Jekyll garden is omitted

Although there is little apparent change, in reality the design has assumed an extra dimension. The flower garden has acquired pillar roses opposite the single herbaceous border, but otherwise plays no part in the metamorphosis of idea that has taken place. We plunge deeply into the world-dominant culture and record (a) a *sense of power* expressed in the floral circle (or fast spinning wheel) and the replacement of the clock with an aviary, and (b) an *uncertainty* expressed subconsciously in the sinister modern version of realistic rock gardens of the time.

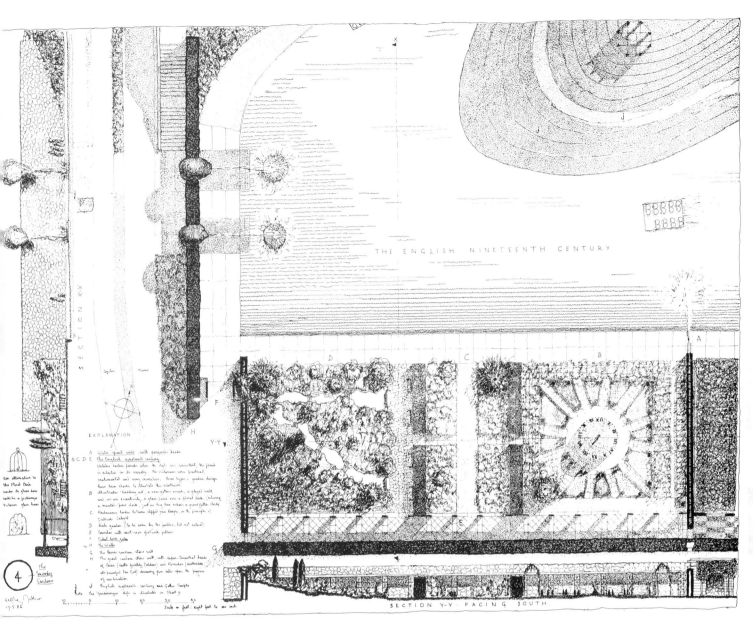

The English Nineteenth Century; the original plan, page 45

For the first time in history the gardens of the Victorian era were not unified in style, and this suggests the rise of a self-determining middle class and the beginnings of democracy. The garden styles chosen range between extreme classicism and romanticism, with the herbaceous border thrown in for good measure. The designs are pleasurable and superficial.

Above, the great aviary at Dropmore, Buckinghamshire, c1850. Below, trellis at Dropmore. (Both illustrations from *The Book of Garden Ornament* by Peter Hunt)

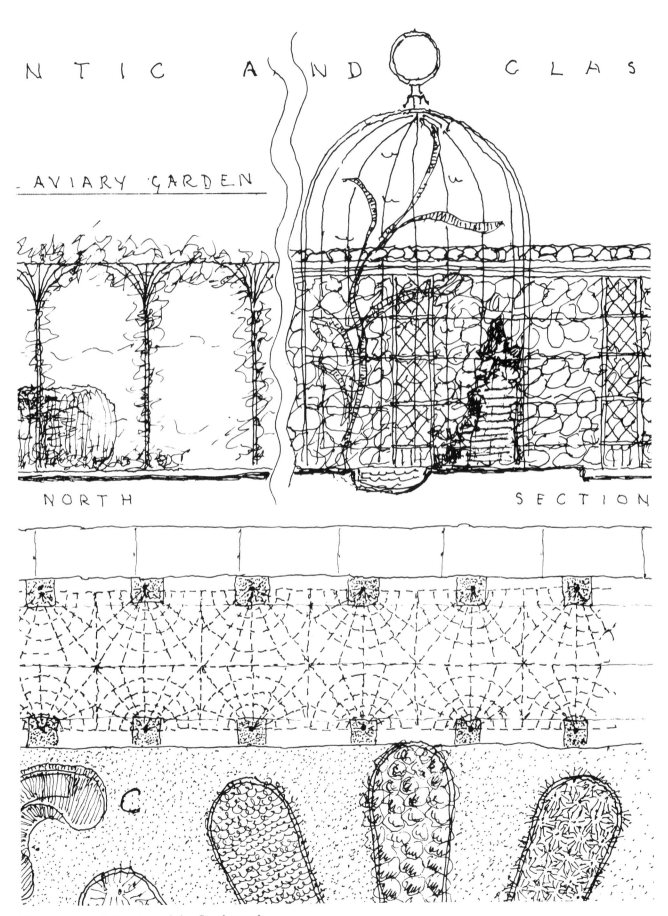

AVIARY GARDEN

NORTH · SECTION

C

The aviary and the plan of the floral arcade

Above, design for flower garden at Ashridge, Buckinghamshire, by Humphry Repton, early nineteenth century. (From *Repton's Handbook of Gardening* by J C Loudon.) Below, topiary at Levens Hall, Cumbria, as existing at the end of the nineteenth century and originally planted in the seventeenth century. (From *Creating Topiary* by Geraldine Lacey)

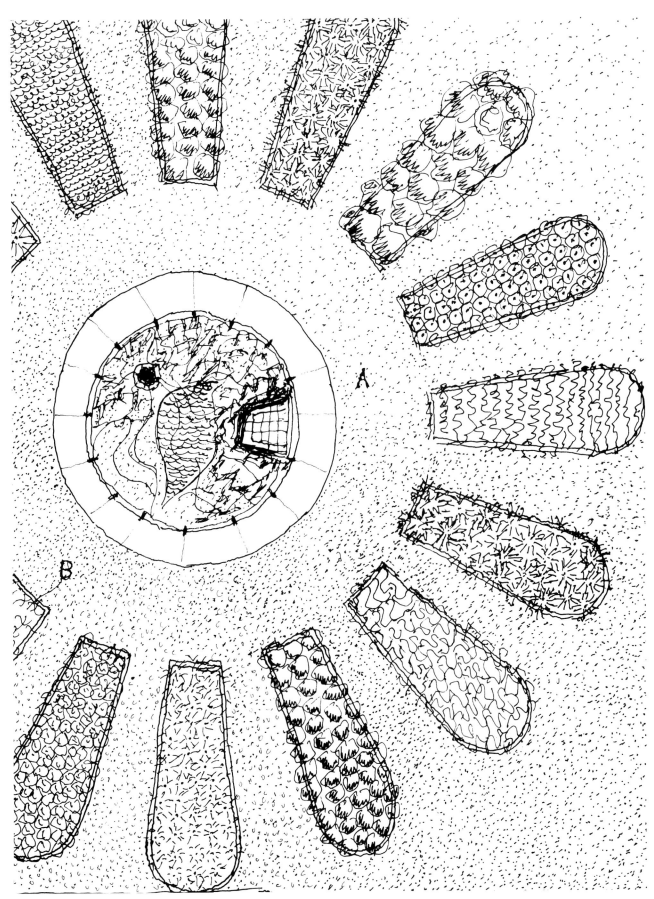

The aviary and the floral circle

Wrong way of forming rock-garden.

Right.

Alpine Plants growing at the bottom of a sloping ridge.

Alpine Plant on border surrounded by half-buried stones.

Corner of a ledge of natural rock with Alpine Plants.

Steps from deep recess of Rock-garden, mossed over with Alpine Flowers.

Ledge of Alpine Flowers (a Garden Sketch).

A page from *The English Flower Garden* by William Robinson, 1883

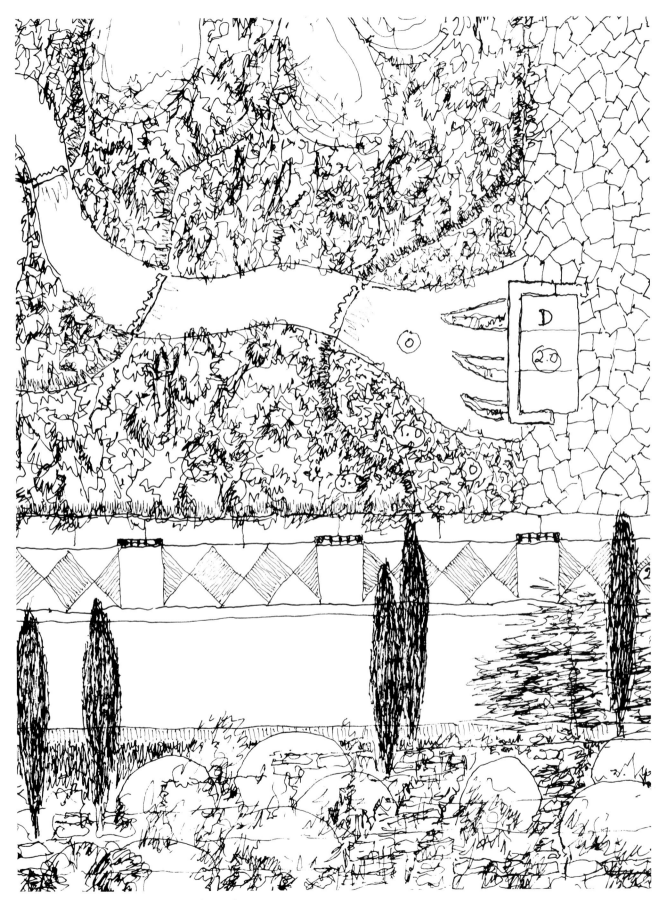

Plan and section through the rock garden

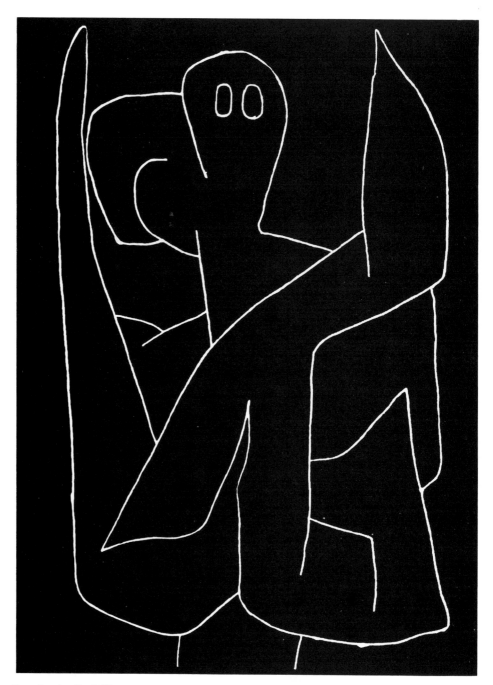

Drawing by Paul Klee

To the intellect the drawing above is unintelligible; the appeal is to the subconscious. Such art was the inspiration for the bodiless water figure among the boulders opposite. Note the head with its bubble-fountain eyes, the beard cascade, the long arms with fingers clutching the balconies. It will not be consciously recognisable as such to the visitor, but subsconsciously it will. It symbolises the uncertainty lying beneath the Victorian high civilisation.

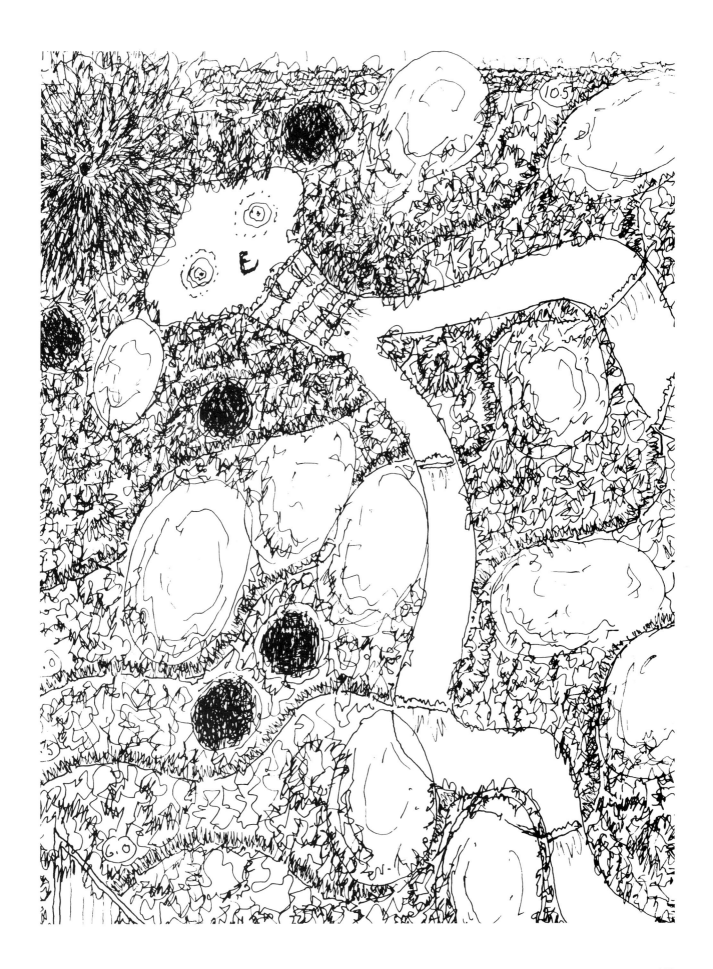

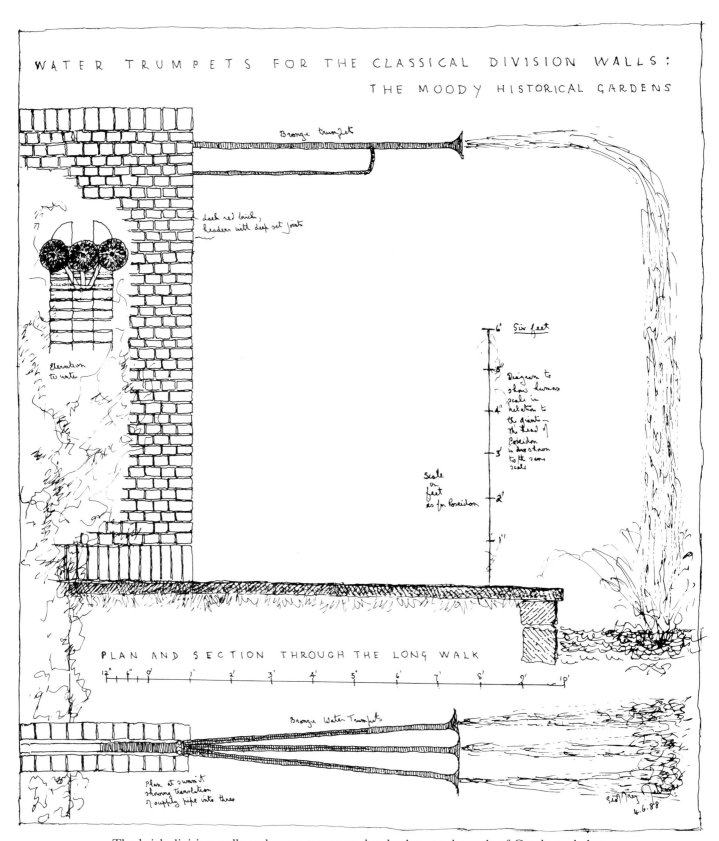

The brick division walls and water trumpets that lead up to the gods of Greek mythology

THE BRONZE HEAD OF POSEIDON

Drawn to the same scale as the water trumpets, this gigantic terror-provoking head of the god Poseidon, hostile to man, will be accompanied by the goddess Demeter, friendly to man. Said Joanna Hoare, aged ten, upon seeing the drawing for the first time: "If I came upon it suddenly I should be startled", but not, she added, if she had come upon it gradually. Parents may be reassured, and all god-fearing adults too.

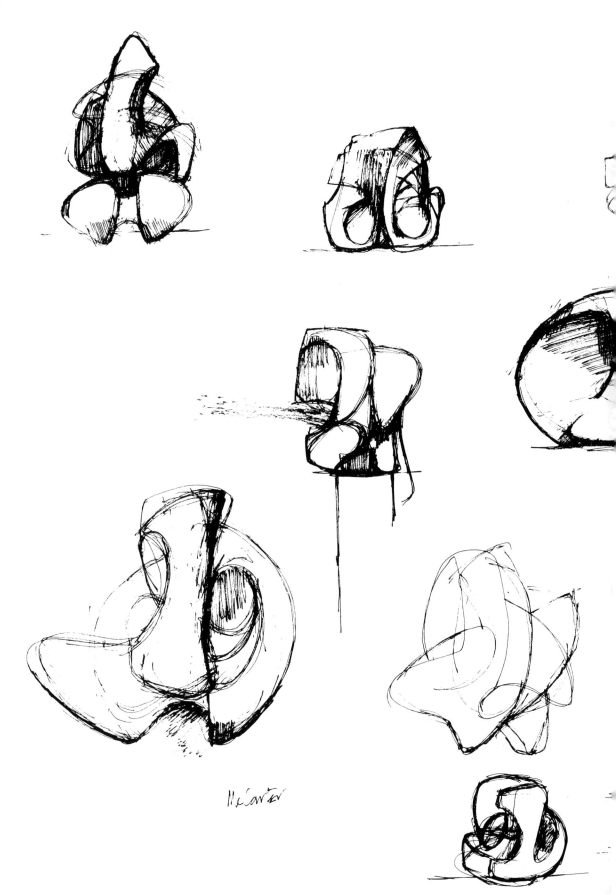

A sheet of sketches for Poseiden by the sculptor Keith McCarter

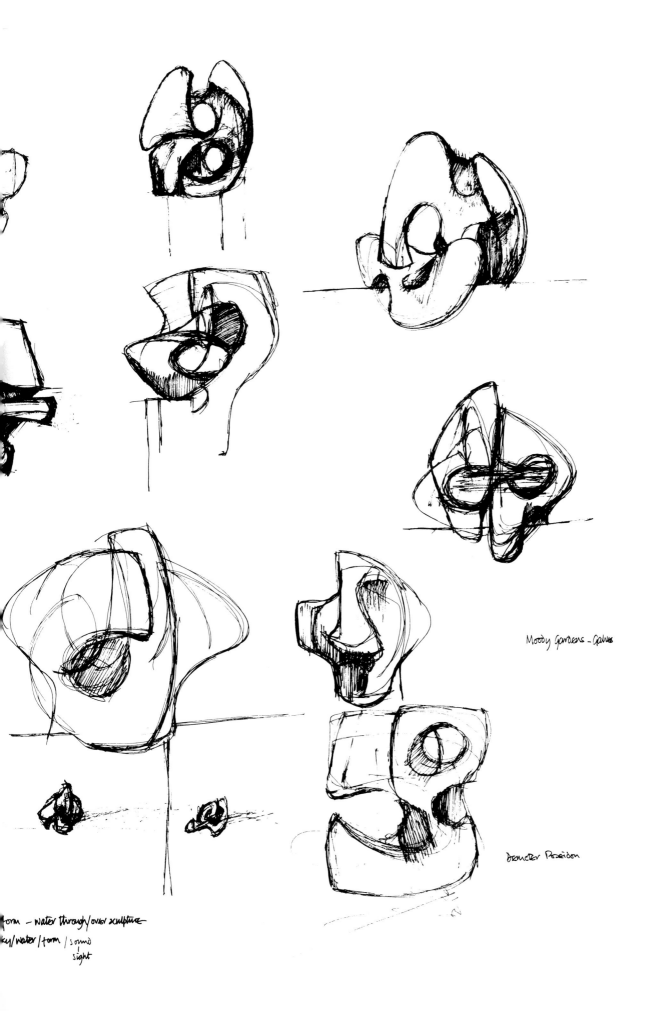

Moody Gardens - Galves

Bronctor Poseidon

form – water through/over sculpture

ky/water/form / sound
sight

BLACK AND WHITE ILLUSTRATIONS

ACKNOWLEDGEMENTS

Without the encouragement and confidence in the project by the Trustees of the Moody Foundation, these designs for the Historical Gardens would neither have begun nor, as anticipated, been brought to reality. Nor would the concept have existed at all without the personal enthusiasm and understanding of Peter Atkins, Director of Horticulture; nor this book published without that of Geraldine Andrews, of the Garden Art Press.

Professional Nominations to Date

David Smith and Keiji Asakura (Houston), executive landscape architects; Marion Thomson (London), plant research; Keith McCarter (Norfolk, England), sculptor, the Gods' heads; Angela Conner (London), sculptor, the Moss Apple; Maggie Keswick (London), consultant China; Keiji Asakura (Houston), consultant Japan; Christine Roussel Inc (New York), artist, Pompeian wall; Michael Spens (Fife, Scotland), arts adviser.

Photographic Work

Peter Greenhalf, England
Moody Gardens, USA

Art Work

Jane Porteous, England

A Note on the Drawings

The original drawings were planned, in May 1985, to be fitted together to form a single picture some 12 feet square on the walls of the reception area at The Moody Gardens.

BIBLIOGRAPHY

The project is basically that of *The Landscape of Man* translated into reality (*The Landscape of Man*, Geoffrey and Susan Jellicoe, Thames and Hudson). A selection from the designer's own library of additional works studied is as follows:

Prehistoric
The Times Atlas of the World
J Hawkes & L Wooley, *Pre-History and the Beginnings of Civilization*
S Piggott, *The Dawn of Civilization*
S Giedion, *The Eternal Present*
F Windels, *The Lascaux Cave Paintings*
G J Campbell, *The Way of Animal Powers*

Egypt, 1500 BC
Baines/Whitehouse, *Oxford Companion to Gardens*
Banister Fletcher, *A History of Architecture*
M L Gothein, *A History of Garden Art*
J S Berrall, *The Garden*
N T Newton, *Design on the Land*
J & R Oldham, *Gardens in Time*
Janson, *A History of Art*

Classical Rome
Banister Fletcher, *A History of Architecture*
M L Gothein, *A History of Garden Art*
Boethius/Ward Perkins, *Roman Architecture*
B W Cuncliffe, *Oxford Companion to Gardens*
J S Berrall, *The Garden*
G Masson, *Italian Gardens*
S Buion, *Pompeii*

Islam
S Crowe et al, *The Gardens of Mughal India*
J & R Oldham, *Gardens in Time*
J S Berrall, *The Garden*
J Lebiman, *Oxford Companion to Gardens*
M L Gothein, *A History of Garden Art*

Mediaeval Europe
Frank Crisp, *Medieval Gardens*
M L Gothein, *A History of Garden Art*
John Harvey, *Medieval Gardens*
J S Berrall, *The Garden*

The Italian Renaissance

Sheperd and Jellicoe, *Italian Gardens of the Renaissance*
G Masson, *Italian Gardens*
M J Darnall, *Oxford Companion to Gardens*
M L Gothein, *A History of Garden Art*
Heydenreich & Lotz, *Architecture in Italy*
N T Newton, *Design on the Land*
Banister Fletcher, *A History of Architecture*

Seventeenth Century France

J S Berrall, *The Garden*
H M Fox, *André le Nôtre*
M L Gothein, *A History of Garden Art*
J & R Oldham, *Gardens in Time*
W M Adams, *The French Gardens 1500-1800*
R Wright, *The Story of Gardening*
K Woodbridge, *Oxford Companion to Gardens*

Nineteenth Century England

J C Loudon, *Landscape Gardening*
Alicia Amherst, *A History of Gardens in England*
Peter Hunt, *The Book of Garden Ornament*
W Robinson, *The English Flower Garden*
Coutts, Osborn & Edwards, *The Complete Book of Gardening*
Reginald Farrer, *The English Rock Garden*

Eighteenth Century Romantic

Dorothy Stroud, *Capability Brown*
Christopher Hussey, *English Gardens and Landscapes*
J D Hunt & Peter Willis, *The Genius of the Place*
K Woodbridge, *Landscape of Antiquity*
M L Gothein, *A History of Garden Art*
J & R Oldham, *Gardens in Time*

China

Arnold Silcock, *An Introduction to Chinese Art and History*
Maggie Keswick, *The Chinese Garden*
Osvald Siren, *The Gardens of China*
Dorothy Graham, *Chinese Gardens*
Lin Yutang, *Imperial Peking*
L Sickman & A Soper, *The Art and Architecture of China*

Japan

Bradley Smith, *Japan, A History of Art*
Kuck Loraine, *The World of Japanese Gardens*
J Conder, *Landscape Gardening in Japan*
Yukio Futagawa, *The Roots of Japanese Architecture*
Ito, Teiji and Takiji Iwajima, *The Japanese Garden, An Approach to Nature*
P T Paine & A Soper, *The Art and Architecture of Japan*

INDEX

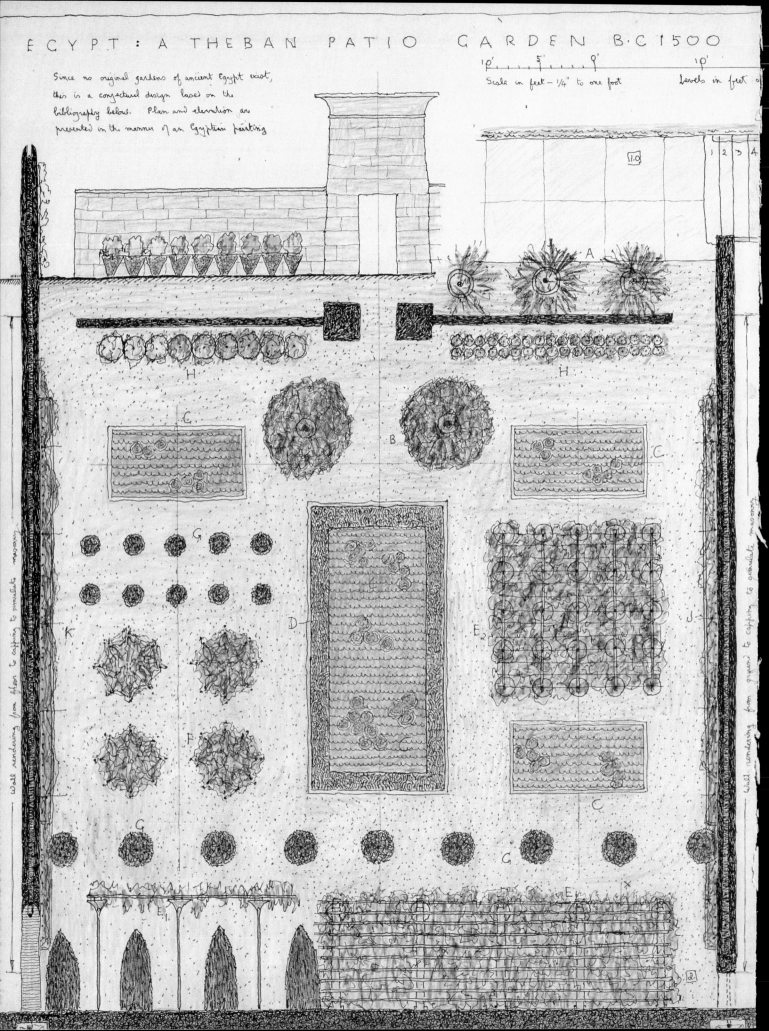

EGYPT: A THEBAN PATIO GARDEN B.C. 1500

Since no original gardens of ancient Egypt exist, this is a conjectural design based on the bibliography below. Plan and elevation are presented in the manner of an Egyptian painting

Scale in feet — 1/4" to one foot   Levels in feet